European Economic and Political Issues, III

European Economic and Political Issues, III

FRANK COLUMBUS
EDITOR

Nova Science Publishers, Inc.
Huntington, New York

Senior Editors:	Susan Boriotti and Donna Dennis
Office Manager:	Annette Hellinger
Graphics:	Wanda Serrano
Information Editor:	Tatiana Shohov
Book Production:	Cathy DeGregory, Lynette Van Helden and Jennifer Vogt
Circulation:	Ave Maria Gonzalez, Ron Hedges and Andre Tillman

Library of Congress Cataloging-in-Publication Data

Available upon request

ISBN 1-56072-908-2

Copyright 2001 by Nova Science Publishers, Inc.
227 Main Street, Suite 100
Huntington, New York 11743
Tele. 631-424-6682 Fax 631-424-4666
e-mail: Novascience@earthlink.net
Web Site: http://www.nexusworld.com/nova

Printed in the United States of America

CONTENTS

PREFACE

This series is intended to provide a forum for substantial research contributions dealing with current political and economic developments in Western Europe. The papers have been selected for their quality, relevance and timeliness. The coherence of each book rests in its fit within the larger framework of the series and its goals.

Chapter 1

THE EUROPEAN UNION'S EASTWARD EXPANSION

Robert C. Rickards
The International University in Germany
Bruchsal, Germany
and
Harz University of Applied Sciences
Wernigerode, Germany

ABSTRACT

The European Union (EU) has agreed to begin accession negotiations with 13 additional countries. This expansion has precedents in earlier attempts to unite Europe. Problems stemming from the candidate members' differing levels of socioeconomic and political development, though, pose considerable challenges to the EU. In particular, Turkey's candidacy has important implications for European statesmen. However, enlargement of the European Union also will affect its territorial organization, need for a common defense, and efforts to achieve closer political integration. The Union's response to these challenges likely will be to continue with its policy of gradual development.

INTRODUCTION

The eastward expansion of the European Union (EU) began in 1989. At that time, its members promised that, having freed themselves from the Soviet Union's shackles, the East European countries could "return to Europe". For their part, Poland and the Baltic countries, Hungary and the Czech Republic, Slovakia and Slovenia insisted that they were not returning to Europe, but had belonged to the Latin-Christian, European community for more than 1000 years.[1]

---

[1] "In der Warteschlange: Die Osterweiterung der EU ist ein gigantisches Unterfangen. Es darf nicht verzögert werden", Christian Schmidt-Häuer, *Die Zeit*, 21. Oktober 1999, p. 3.

For that reason, this article begins with a brief description of the historical background behind the EU's prospective enlargement. Next, it presents selected characteristics of the candidate countries and examines the special case of Turkey. The article then takes up the question of where the Union's borders lie, discusses strategic considerations associated with the border question, and analyzes the geopolitical consequences of membership growth. It explains both the advantages and disadvantages of further expansion as the EU's preferred foreign policy instrument. After arguing the need for institutional reforms prior to the accession of any new members, the article closes with some thoughts about the Union's likely future development.

HISTORICAL BACKGROUND

More than 1200 years ago, in 799, Charlemagne and Pope Leo III met in Paderborn. An epic centered on this meeting refers to the King of the Franks as the "Father of Europe" (*pater europae*). Admittedly, the Frankish realm did not encompass anywhere near all of present-day Europe. Still, beginning with Charlemagne, the ambition arose to unite all of Europe. Pursuit of that goal initially took the form of German expansion and colonization, together with subjugation of the Slavic tribes. However, its subsequent course was neither entirely martial nor merely a process of Germanization. On the contrary, the colonists from Western Europe who settled in the East also cleared the land and built cities. In doing so, they consolidated the region and integrated it into the European "world economy" of those times.

Accordingly, the East's first adaptation to Western notions of law was its acceptance of the *ius teutonicum*. That was not a German legal code, but rather a body of law for settlers' putting down roots in the eastern "New Europe". In addition, the historic legacy of this early eastward expansion included the rights of free cities. Known as the Magdeburg Law, more than 80 other cities subsequently adopted it. Together with the *ius teutonicum*, it thus became the prevailing basis of written law in both middle and eastern Europe.

Besides such laws, the West's eastward expansion brought with it technological know-how, beginning for example, with the introduction of the iron plow. Furthermore, for centuries German served as the region's *lingua franca*. At the same time, the East Europeans' western neighbors were almost exclusively Germans.

Proximity to the Slavs likewise greatly enriched German culture. The nation of *Dichter und Denker* would have been much poorer without this intellectual cross-fertilization. The works of Kant and Schopenhauer, Gryphius and Hauptmann, Rilke and Werfel, Kafka and Kisch, Celan and Canetti – and even today of Günter Grass from Danzig and Fritz Stern from Breslau (Wrocwlaw) – are examples of such intercultural interaction.

Consequently, many proponents of the EU wax enthusiastic when they reflect on Europe's rise, its eastward expansion, and its secular change from a community of faith (*res publica christiana*) in the Middle Ages to, as Voltaire termed it in 1751, "a kind of great Republic". While this republic seems to have included neither the Islamic Turks nor the Russians and the Serbs, it had no clearly defined borders. So, until the present day, the question of where Europe ends has had no definitive answer.

Many Europeans believe the 19th century nation-state, in contrast, badly damaged well-established, interwoven, cultural and commercial relationships.[2] In the 20th century, the aggression and genocide practiced by Germany under National Socialism rent asunder and destroyed these relationships in a previously unimaginable way.[3]

After World War II, the Marshal Plan, the Breton Woods Agreement, the North Atlantic Treaty Organization, and the European Coal and Steel Community (ECSC) laid the foundation for a new order in Western Europe. As conceived by its founding fathers, Robert Schumann and Jean Monnet, the ECSC excluded countries within what then was the Soviet sphere of influence. Consequently, in the east, the Community extended only to the upper reaches of the Elbe River. When the EU did open itself, it first was to the west (England, Ireland, and Denmark in 1973), next to the south (Greece, in 1981, Spain and Portugal, in 1985), and then to the neutrals (Austria, Sweden, and Finland in 1995).

Following communism's collapse, though, the newly reunited Germany no longer wanted to be on the EU's eastern fringe. A broad consensus formed there, that the Oder River should not become like the Rio Grande: a river of money launderers, drug smugglers, illegal immigrants, and white slave traders. Therefore, in the years after 1989, Chancellors Helmut Kohl and Gerhard Schröder committed themselves steadfastly to expanding the EU eastward. Despite growing opposition from its state governments and complaints about being the "paymaster" of Europe, no West European country stands to profit more from that expansion than Germany. For example, since 1993, Germany's surpluses from trade with middle and eastern Europe have more than doubled. No wonder that the Association of German Industry's East European Committee values the region so highly both as a consumer and supplier market![4]

Meanwhile, Germany in particular and the EU generally have been subject to the forces of migration, monetarization, and globalization. Although having grown from 6 to 15 members, the EU's leaders have tried to deal with these forces within the Community's original institutional structures. In part due to the inadequacy of those institutions, the agreements hammered out in Maastricht, Amsterdam, and Kopenhagen have remained largely technocratic piecework. Increasingly ineffective, the Union is ill-prepared either to restore or stabilize Eastern Europe. Furthermore, had the United States not insisted repeatedly that, at least in Bosnia and Kosovo, the West Europeans coordinate their policies, then even today they likely would be reacting defensively and disunitedly to the historic challenges facing them. Only gradually have EU-leaders come

---

[2] "Joschka Fischer: Der Föderalist", Jochen Buchsteiner, *Die Zeit*, 21. Juni 2000, p. 14.

[3] The French Interior Minister and the German Foreign Minister recently traded views on the nation-state, Germany under National Socialism, and a possible federal structure for a united Europe. See "Streitgespäch Joschka Fischer contra Jean-Pierre Chevènement", *Die Zeit*, 21. Juni 2000, pp. 13-18.

[4] "Schröder Cruises Eastern Shores of the Baltic", Jasper von Altenbockum, *Frankfurter Allgemeine Zeitung*, (English Edition), June 6, 2000, p. 1.

to recognize the wisdom in the remark of the Czech Republic's President Václav Havel: "If the West doesn't stabilize the East, the East will destabilize the West."

The most effective form of stabilization for both is the EU's expansion eastward. Besides socioeconomic benefits and enhanced security, it offers the opportunity to reform the Community's institutions and to define Europe's borders.

THE CANDIDATE COUNTRIES AND THEIR PROBLEMS

Recognizing these facts, the EU again has opened itself for new members. A special summit meeting in 1999 in Tampere, Portugal, began with a report on the progress six East European countries had made in bringing their legal codes into conformance with EU law. "As a consequence of the dramatic changes in Europe and especially in the aftermath of the Kosovo War", though, the EU-Commission then decided to begin accession negotiations with six more candidate countries in eastern and southern Europe during 2000. In addition, it also formally placed Turkey on the list of candidate countries, although accession negotiations with it will start somewhat later.

Thus, after Poland, the Czech Republic, Hungary, Slovenia, Estonia and Cyprus, which have been working hard to adapt their legal systems to the 31 chapters and 80,000 pages of European law (*acquis communautaire*), a second group of countries has stepped out of the waiting line and approached the negotiating table. They are Latvia, Lithuania, Slovakia, Bulgaria, Rumania and Malta. Table 1 contains descriptive data for these 12 countries and Turkey.

Table 1: Selected Characteristics of Old and New Candidates for EU-Membership

	Variable				
Country	Area (km^2)	Population (Mio.)	Per Capita Purchasing Power (€)	Inflation Rate (%)	Unemploy-ment Rate (%)
Estonia	45,227	1,4	7,300	8,2	9,7
Cyprus	9,251	0,7	14,787	2,2	3,3
Czech Republic	78,866	10,3	12,200	10,7	6,5
Hungary	93,030	10,1	9,800	14,3	7,8
Poland	312,685	38,7	7,800	11,8	10,6
Slovenia	20,253	2,0	13,700	7,9	7,9
Bulgaria	110,994	8.3	4,600	22,3	16,0
Latvia	64,589	2,4	5,500	4,7	13,8
Lithuania	65,301	3,7	6,200	5,1	13,3
Malta	315,6	0,4	n.a.	2,4	5,1
Rumania	238,391	22,5	5,500	59,1	6,3
Slovak Republic	49,034	5,4	9,300	6,7	12,5
Turkey	780,580	64,6	6,200	n.a.	11,1

As the table shows, Poland has by far the largest territory and population among the 12 countries, while Cyprus, Slovenia, and the Czech Republic have the highest per capita incomes. Just Cyprus and Malta, however, have both low inflation and low unemployment. Today, probably only Malta could hope to withstand the pressure of economic competition emanating from the EU-countries. The inflation rates for Bulgaria and Rumania suggest that economically neither really is prepared for serious accession negotiations. Still, the EU chose to reward them for their political solidarity during the conflict in Kosovo by inviting both countries to begin negotiations.

Most East European governments have given thorough liberalization of their economies the highest priority. In contrast, the level of their other activities, especially in the welfare policy area, has declined markedly, despite the high social costs of economic reform. So far, EU-reports have made scant mention of these costs. But East European governments nevertheless have to deal with them. In Poland, for example, miners, steelworkers, and nurses have laid siege to government ministries. Furthermore, Polish farmers have interrupted the West-to-East flow of goods in order to keep EU-subsidized agricultural imports out of their country.

Overall, East European governments already have accomplished much. Besides adopting EU-laws and regulations, they have opened their markets, freed their prices, and allowed provocative disequalities in the distribution of incomes to arise. Yet prior to accession, the new candidates for EU-membership must satisfy three preconditions set forth in 1993 in Copenhagen: stable political institutions; respect for human rights; and a functioning market economy that can withstand competition. Due to the large structural, economic, and legal differences among them, the candidate countries therefore will not be able to join the EU simultaneously.

Particularly in such areas as the free flow of capital, worker mobility, and residency rights, as well as agricultural, environmental, and legal policy, all candidate member countries still have much work to do.[5] In addition, poorer EU-members, such as Spain, Portugal, and Greece, want to limit the East European countries' access to the Community's structural development funds. For their part, richer EU-members fear that East Europeans will flood their labor markets.[6] These fears are not unjustified when one considers that per capita income in some of the candidate countries is just 30% of the EU mean. In fact, the Dutch economy alone is larger than the economies of all the accession candidates together. Over and above the economic and social costs of further expansion, many EU-citizens also fear it could dilute the Community's values a and weaken its institutions.

Consequently, the Finns, the French, and the Spaniards have reined in the new EU-Commission President Romano Prodi and the German Foreign Minister Joschka Fischer.

---

[5] "Baltics Struggle to Head West, But Face Countervailing Winds", Jasper von Altenbockum, *Frankfurter Allgemeine Zeitung*, (English Edition), May 9, 2000, p. 3.

[6] "Neue Ökonomie, altes Europa: Am Erfolg des Lissabonner Beschäftigungsgipfels sind Zweifel erlaubt", Christian Wernicke, *Die Zeit*, 23. März 2000, p. 33.

Both Prodi and Fischer had been pushing early admission for some candidate countries.[7] However, the latest EU-report now states that the candidates' preparations will be examined closely. Thus, even the leading candidate country, Hungary, unlikely will have its accession ratified before 2004. Other candidate members will have to be satisfied with more extended transition periods.

Nevertheless, the EU values all the candidate members as buffer states. With technological support from the EU, they now help to shield Western Europe from asylum seekers and organized crime. As compensation, they have received somewhat easier access to the European internal market. But the EU still retains a well-developed system of tariffs and quotas for almost all East European agricultural products. In contrast, the great speed with which West European exporters have captured market share in Eastern Europe indicates that, to date, freer trade chiefly benefits the EU.[8]

So, just as Germans 150 years ago were divided between one group seeking a larger solution to the question of unification and a second group favoring a smaller German state, a larger concept of Europe today competes with the notion of a smaller, "core Europe". Surely, one can not dismiss the critics' arguments easily. But need the EU really fear expansion costs that might total 150 billion DM? The Federal Republic of Germany alone spends that amount to subsidize the state governments and infrastructure in the former East Germany. As for the dreaded flood of migrant workers, that fear also arose before the accession of Spain. The nightmare visions, though, never materialized. Following its accession, Spain's economy boomed, keeping most Spaniards at home. There is no *a priori* reason to suspect that the East European candidate countries will develop differently.

TURKEY

Turkey, on the other hand, is a special case – and that not only due to its large territory and population size (see Table 1).[9] This NATO-partner finally has received the status it had sought since the 1963 Association Agreement between Ankara and the then European Economic Community. The EU summit conference in Helsinki now has elevated Turkey to candidate member. Many analysts see that as an historic opportunity.[10] In contrast, some observers believe it could be the beginning of the end of Europe's political union.

---

[7] "Jump-Starting Europe", Günther Nonnemacher, *Frankfurter Allgemeine Zeitung*, (English Edition), May 23, 2000, p. 1.

[8] Nevertheless businesses are increasingly cautious about admitting new members to the Community. "In Germany, Firms Call for Slower EU Expansion", Barry James, *International Herald Tribune*, April 26, 2000, p. 1.

[9] "Ungleich unter Gleichen: Der EU-Kandidat Türkei bleibt ein Sonderfall", Joachim Fritz-Vannahme, *Die Zeit*, 16. Dezember 1999, p. 10.

[10] "Wer Staaten wie die Türkei draußen lässt, vertut eine historische Chance", Theo Sommer, *Die Zeit*, 9. Dezember 1999, p. 1.

For most European security policymakers, Turkey's candidate membership represents an historic opportunity. For decades, they have wanted to secure Europe's southern flank and stabilize the crisis region between the Persian Gulf and the Caucasus. By instrumentalizing Turkey to do so, they consciously are extending Europe's borders beyond Europe itself. Although the idea seems foolhardy to many other analysts, security policy considerations may afford an argument for Turkish membership in the European Union in order to halt the advance of certain nationalist or Islamic movements. But the European Union is not the North Atlantic Treaty Organization. At present, it has different functions and responsibilities. For a European *policy* in light of the goal of socioeconomic, political, and cultural integration, Turkish membership, argue critics, could be a disaster.[11]

That touches on fears for Europe's political union. If Turkey joins the European Club, Iraq, Iran, Armenia, and Azerbaijan suddenly will become Europe's neighbors. Turkey at best has ticklish relations with all of them, no different from its relations with EU-member Greece, candidate member Cyprus, Syria or Russia. Indeed, one could term Turkish foreign policy a "360°-nightmare". This state of affairs could hamper seriously formation of a common European foreign policy.

Likewise critics object variously to the military's influence on Turkish politics, frequent human rights violations, and differences stemming from the country's Islamic/Middle Eastern culture. Moreover, they fear that millions more Turkish workers will migrate to Western Europe, where wages five or ten times higher than those paid at home will tempt them to settle permanently.[12] In fact, 2.5 million people of Turkish origin already make their home in Germany alone.

Yet no European leader wants to initiate accession negotiations with Ankara before it begins to protect human rights very carefully. In addition, accession negotiations to the Community may serve as a lever to obtain a solution to the Cyprus question in the form of a federation or confederation. A Turkey, freed of the military's involvement in the government and fulfilling the Copenhagen criteria certainly should belong to Europe, say proponents.[13]

In any event, Turkish accession and extension of the future common European foreign and security policies to the borders of Syria, Iraq, Iran and the Caucasus region are not immediate priorities for the EU. Until it puts its domestic and foreign affairs in order, and there is an agreement between Ankara and Brussels limiting Turkish labor mobility, it is likely that Turkey will continue to be only an economic associate on the fringe of the European Community.

---

[11] "Braucht Europa Grenzen?: Die EU muss ihre Türen schließen, zum Beispiel für die Türkei", Joachim Fritz-Vannahme, *Die Zeit*, 9. Dezember 1999, p. 1.

[12] Time to Slow Down and Consolidate Around 'Euro-Europe', Valéry Giscard d'Estaing and Helmut Schmidt, *International Herald Tribune*, April 11, 2000, p. 8. Also, "EU Warned of Crisis Looming: Elder Statesmen Call for Reforms, Caution on Enlargement", *Frankfurter Allgemeine Zeitung* (English Edition), April 11, 2000, p. 2.

[13] "Schluss mit der Erbsenzählerei!: Die Türkei will in die EU – wie zwölf weitere Staaten. Kann Europa das verkraften? Ein ZEIT-Gespräch mit EU-Kommissar Günter Verheugen", Joachim Fritz-Vannahme und Christian Wernicke, *Die Zeit*, 9. Dezember 1999, p. 6.

EUROPE'S BORDERS

Even to many committed Europeans, the goal of admitting another 12 or 13 members appears to be an example of imperial overstretch that makes excessive demands on the EU's current capabilities. Just imagining an internal market with 500 million consumers requires considerable vision. How will it be possible to develop uniform standards for such a vast region with so many diverse cultures?[14]

Fortunately, surrounding seas limit Europe naturally in the north, west, and south. To the east, though, the Eurasian continent opens like the top of a funnel. During the Cold War with its division of Germany and the Continent, the EU needed to remain open to the east. Accordingly, neither in the 1957 Treaty of Rome nor in its ambitious extensions, the Maastricht and Amsterdam agreements, is there any mention of the Community's borders.[15]

However, the Cold War ended over a decade ago and Europe subsequently has begun taking on a new shape. Some opponents of EU expansion now believe that whoever seeks still more from the Union likely will get less. Regardless of its cumbersome institutions and complicated regulations, their ambition for the EU is not to have merely a large domestic market with a common currency. They want common agricultural, defense, economic, foreign, and social policies too. Formulating such policies, they argue, demands concentrated effort on the possible. Many EU-citizens already have difficulties accepting the prospective expansion that eventually will include twelve new members. Some formerly pro-EU politicians have started to backpeddle because voters are switching to anti-EU parties and candidates such as the Austrian xenophobe Haider and the French ultra-nationalist Le Pen.[16] In the candidate countries, many people fear economic rationalization. East European governments, like that of Jerzy Buzek in Poland, have legitimized themselves by promising their voters early EU-membership. Meanwhile, West European export industries have ripped away marketshare from East European firms. The promised stability through prosperity therefore has not

---

[14] An interesting recent example of this cultural diversity has been the debate over opening the military services to women. See "Europas Richter als Feldherren", Niklaus Blome, *Frankfurter Allgemeine Zeitung*, 10. Januar 2000; and "Berufsverbot vor Gericht: Zwingen Europas Richter die Bundeswehr, Frauen an die Waffen zu lassen?", Constanze Stelzenmüller, *Die Zeit*, 5. Januar 2000, p. 6.

[15] "Spiel ohne Grenzen: Was Europa ist, wurde lange Zeit nur durch Inhalte definiert. Nun ist auch politische Geografie gefragt", Joachim Fritz-Vannahme, *Die Zeit*, 20. Januar 2000, p. 37.

[16] "Taube Ohren und leere Rhetorik: Vor dem Lissabonner Gipfel: Europas Reaktionen auf Haiders Erfolg bringt die schlimmsten Defekte der EU zum Vorschein", Tony Judt, *Die Zeit*, 23. März 2000, pp. 10-11; "Bann über Österreich?: Wo die Freiheit in Gefahr ist, muss sich Europa einmischen", Matthias Nass and "Europa leistet sich aus moralischen Gründen eine große Heuchelei", Theo Sommer, *Die Zeit*, 10. Februar 2000, p. 1; "Angst vor Haider?: Der Machtwechsel in Österreich verändert Europa", Werner A. Perger, *Die Zeit*, 3. Februar 2000, p. 1; "Noch nicht der Ernstfall: Warum sich EU-Kommissionspräsident Prodi bei der Strafaktion gegen Österreich zurückhält", Joachim Fritz-Vannahme, *Die Zeit*, 3. Februar 2000, p. 6; and "Austria Part of EU, Schuessel Insists", *International Herald Tribune*, February 9, 2000, p. 7.

materialized.[17] So, anti-EU politicians, for example the Polish peasantry's champion Lepper, have gained support in the candidate countries too.[18]

Opponents of further EU expansion dread a popular backlash within the member countries. If the EU is not to degenerate into a balkanized, bureaucratic, barely governable organization, they argue, it must remain capable of acting to achieve its *political* ambition. In order to make the most out of its diversity, the EU thus finally must decide where its borders lie.

The EU recently has hinted to Russia and North Africa that they must remain outside. Russia belongs to Europe, but not to the European Union. For that, it simply is too large and too involved in Eurasian entanglements. It could be a partner, but not a member in the Club. Consquently, Russia and North Africa eventually might be plausible candidates for the status of economic associate.

At the same time, though, the EU has offered the former Yugoslavia and Albania a "perspective on membership", for the event that both sides recognize their mutual borders and respective national minorities' rights. These are preconditions that, for the foreseeable future, they are unlikely to meet. Furthermore, it would be unwise suddenly to expose the fragile economies of those countries to full market competition with Western Europe's highly developed enterprises. The rapid demise of most of the former East Germany's industry is a case in point.

But despite the tentative "no" to Russia and North Africa, the "yes" to Turkey, together with Yugoslavia's and Albania's "perspective on membership", still leaves the European project open-ended. Are Croatia, Bosnia, Macedonia, or an eventually independent Montenegro any less "European"? Or Belarus, Moldavia, and the ethnically splittered Ukraine? And beyond Turkey, Armenia, Azerbaidjan, Georgia, Kazakstan, Kirghizstan, and Turkmenistan are waiting in line. "Then why not admit South Korea?", ask the critics. After all, it already has a market economy, political democracy, and guarantees human and minority rights.

So just where will the Union's borders ultimately will lie? The Community's leaders continue to avoid answering this question, counseling their interlocutors instead quietly to wait and see.

---

[17] "Tiger mit halb vollem Tank", Christian Schmidt-Hauer, *Die Zeit*, 13. April 2000, p. 9.

[18] "So ängstlich ist Suleyken: Nächste Woche berät die EU in Lissabon über die Arbeitslosigkeit in ihren Ländern. Derweil sehen Polens Kleinbauern dem Beitritt ohne Hoffnung entgegen", Christian Schmidt-Häuer, *Die Zeit*, 16. März 2000, p. 3.

STRATEGY

Strategic considerations underlie the Community's unwillingness to define its borders.[19] In the 21st century, the current sole superpower, the United States, likely will be joined by China. Russia still will be a world power despite its inner weaknesses, which will last decades. Japan will remain a financial world power. In addition, India could become a world power because it, just like China, by mid-century will have a population of 1.5 billion people. Brazil also could develop into a world power. Furthermore, the number of countries with nuclear weapons (8) could increase too.[20]

Moreover, almost everywhere in Asia, Africa, and to a certain extent in Latin America, dramatic population growth is occurring. By the middle of the 21st century, there will be six times more people living on earth than at the beginning of the 20th century. The amount of land and water available per person will continue to decrease, conceivably leading to numerous wars. The problems of containing wars and resultant refugee flows, arms control, and development assistance programs will call for international solutions. Meanwhile, the population of most West European countries is declining and with it, potentially, their political influence.

Due to the sharp increase in emission of hothouse gases, global warming presents the frightening prospect of rising oceans. Dealing with it and otherwise maintaining some semblance of adequate global environmental quality, will call for new international rules. Experience suggests that the abovementioned current and likely future world powers egotistically will try to avoid making necessary sacrifices when formulating such rules. One no doubt can expect similar behavior from them with regard to reorganizing world financial markets, limiting nuclear and strategic armaments, and regulating new technologies.

The recent international climate conferences as well as the transnational credit and currency crises of the 1990s demonstrated clearly the future division of power and influence in the world. Neither Belgium nor Italy, neither Poland nor Sweden, neither France nor Germany – none of the European countries alone has sufficient weight to defend its legitimate interests vis à vis the great powers.

So, for the EU, the strategic motive of asserting common national interests is becoming increasingly important. Of course, most Europeans rightly recognize that continued cooperation with the United States is desirable, but they still are chary of being too dependent on the Americans.[21] Many Europeans find neither all American political, social, and economic policies nor cultural concepts to be desirable or useful. Among the Europeans, the French perhaps are noticeably more sensitive in this regard than are, say, the Germans. However, even Germans find the discontinuity and ambiguity of American

---

[19] "Macht ohne Grenzen: Die Erweiterung der EU nach Ost und Süd wird Europa strategisch stärken", Christoph Bertram, *Die Zeit*, 8. Juni 2000, p. 18.

[20] "Strategie der Selbstbehauptung: Trotz aller Krisen und Mängel ist die EU ein großer Erfolg. Das kann auch in Zukunft so bleiben", Helmut Schmidt, *Die Zeit*, 21. Oktober 1999, p. 7.

[21] "Die Reifeprüfung: Vor dem Berliner Gipfel: Europa muss Amerika endlich einholen", Josef Joffe, *Die Zeit*, 31. Mai 2000, p. 1.

foreign policy disturbing: for example, with regard to Russia, China, Islam, or NATO's future responsibilities. For all these reasons, European strategists think it crucial that the Community be able to speak to its ally and friend, the United States, with a common voice.

The strategic motive of common self-assertion already was present fifty years ago with the first efforts at West European cooperation (e.g., the ECSC). At that time, though, two other strategic goals were more important: first, creating a bulwark against further Soviet expansion; and second, restraining and integrating (then, just West) Germany into Western Europe. Following two World Wars, both of these motives arose from concern about maintaining peace in Europe. Today, the anti-Soviet (or anti-Russian) motivation has hardly any significance. Restraining and integrating Germany, though, remains important in the 21st century, due in part to its greater size following reunification. At the same time, the enormous benefits resulting from the EU's economic and monetary union have become an additional strategic motivation for European statesmen. In the 21st century, the self-assertion motive will be equally important.

GEOPOLITICAL CONSEQUENCES

But what geopolitical consequences does a process have, that brings more and more countries into the EU? In order to make the implications of this question clear, imagine the EU not as a group of nation-states, but as a single, traditional nation-state. Then it would be a country that had grown from six states in 1958, to 15 in 1995, and 30 by about 2010 -- from 200 million residents to 350 million today, and tomorrow half a billion! Many analysts would view this nation-state as an aggressive empire, a threat to its neighbors, and a serious challenger to other great powers and the established world order.[22]

The reality of the EU hardly could offer a stronger contrast. Instead of fearing it, the Union's neighbors demand to join it. The sole remaining superpower America not only assisted in its founding, but also repeatedly helped it overcome obstacles in the Community's early years. The US has encouraged, indeed insisted, on the EU's further expansion to include Poland, Estonia, and Turkey. For its part, one-time world power Russia, which so much still wants to be treated like one, objects to NATO's enlargement eastward, but welcomes the EU's expansion up to its very borders![23]

The explanation for this contrast is twofold. First, inwardly, the EU effectively restrains and integrates Germany, making a European Germany instead of a German Europe possible. Second, outwardly, as a genial hybrid of a confederation and a federally organized state, the EU appears benign to both its neighbors and the great powers. The Union radiates material advantages, not power-based threats.

---

[22] "Macht ohne Grenzen", Christoph Bertram, *Die Zeit*, 8. Juni 2000, p. 18.

[23] "NATO Growth Spurt Unlikely by 2002", Joseph Fitchett, *International Herald Tribune*, May 23, 2000, p. 11.

This latter assessment of the European Union, though, underestimates its real power. For the time-being, that continues to work to the Community's advantage. But sooner or later the curtain will rise, revealing even to skeptics the EU's full power potential.

One reason for underestimating the Union has been its lack of military muscle. That now is changing.[24] A former NATO General Secretary, Javier Solana, has become the EU's High Representative for Foreign and Security Policy. Subsequent to his appointment, several EU-countries have agreed by 2003 to raise a force of 60,000 troops that can sustain operations outside the NATO area for at least one year.[25]

However desirable it may be that the heretofore vague European security identity finally becomes a concrete capacity – the Community's international influence no longer depends on it. Instead, with the end of the Cold War, economic factors are proving to be more important than military ones. In this regard, the European Union is a heavyweight.[26] It speaks and acts for its members in all international trade questions. With the Euro's introduction, it has established the world's second most important currency.

Furthermore, in the foreign policy area the member countries are coming closer together too. For example, in the Balkans: 10 years ago the Europeans disagreed among themselves about the right policy for that region. Today, they have sent the largest number of troops, delivered the lion's share of reconstruction assistance, and are responsible for the stability pact, which supposedly will restore the region's economic well-being.[27] Or take the Near East. Here hardly any European state seeks to gain advantage at its neighbors' expense. On the contrary, all EU members have agreed that a viable Palestine and close regional cooperation between Israel and its Arab neighbors are essential for peace. Increasingly, the national foreign policy of member states is only effective through the Union. Thereby, the EU effectively has become a power enhancer of national foreign policy.

If, in spite of such impressive evidence of international influence, the EU still does not appear to be a great power, it perhaps is because "Brussels" does not yet have a geopolitical identity. The more states that want to join the EU, the longer expansion will be its most obvious foreign policy instrument. Correspondingly, its international image will remain fuzzy and its members will be able to avoid assuming a great power's responsibilities.

In a certain phase of its development, expansion thus has proved useful to the EU. Only in this fashion could it function as an ordering factor that contributed to the

---

[24] "U.S. Starts to Fret Over EU Military Independence", Frederick Bonnart, *International Herald Tribune*, May 24, 2000, p. 8.

[25] "Lernt Europa?: Drei Berichte decken Fehler und Schwächen bei den Beteiligten am Kosovo Krieg auf", Constanze Stelzenmüller, *Die Zeit*, p. 9; and "Pflugscharen zu Schwertern: Die EU will lernen, Krisen in Eigenregie zu meistern – notfalls auch mit Soldaten. Amerika gefällt das gar nicht", Constanze Stelzenmüller, *Die Zeit*, 25. November 1999, p. 10.

[26] "Europa im Aufbruch: Die neue Alte Welt könnte dem 21. Jahrhundert ihren Stempel aufdrücken", Theo Sommer, *Die Zeit*, 5. Januar 2000, p. 4.

[27] "Europa muss seine Konflikte selbst lösen: ZEIT-Gespräch mit Christopher Patten, EU-Kommissar für auswärtige Beziehungen, über Krisenprävention und humanitäre Hilfe", Joachim Fritz-Vannahme und Christian Wernicke, *Die Zeit*, 3. Februar 2000, p. 3.

Continent's stabilization. Expansion continues to be the strongest foreign policy instrument it has. That is because on acceptance into the Club, a new member must adopt all the rules previously set by the old members. It renounces its sovereignty in wide areas, as if it were a country occupied by the European Union. Unlike in earlier times, though, the country does not feel itself to be a loser, but rather a victor. The right of participation in collective decision-making more than compensates for the independence lost.

EXPANSION AS A FOREIGN POLICY INSTRUMENT

Expansion has an additional relevant effect. The new member identifies itself with the old ones, while the whole Union thereafter must stand up for the new member. Besides agricultural subsidies, funds to restructure industries and regions, and support of a common currency, that means solidarity with regard to security policy. The latter comes so close to a defense alliance, that it hardly is distinguishable from one.

The various treaty documents do not mention such a defense alliance specifically. That could change in the near future, if portions of the West European Union (WEU) Treaty are inserted into the EU Treaty text. But doing so will create no new duties. Instead, it merely will confirm formally what, after all, is the substance of integration. In comparison to the North Atlantic Treaty, which is "just" a defense treaty, ties within the EU are much denser. If a third party attacked an EU-member country, the whole EU would be at risk.

Thus, every member country shares the EU's external borders. For example, since Finland's accession, the Union, and hence Germany, has a 1,200 km.-long border with Russia. When Poland becomes a member, then Kaliningrad, Belarus, and Ukraine will become immediate neighbors of all EU-states. When Cyprus joins, the EU will become a regional actor in the Near East. Every conflict in western and central Asia will affect and challenge the Union when it admits Turkey. Expansion therefore has strategic consequences for all EU-members.

Many people ignore this secret alliance aspect of the Union. They treat the issue of expansion as if it involved nothing more than enlargement of the Common Market. Consequently, they overlook the fact that expanding the Union's geographic base means increased geopolitical responsibility for its members. So the Union rightly demands that candidate members resolve all border disputes with their neighbors prior to accession. When the heads of government late last year added Turkey to the list of candidate countries, they insisted that by 2004 Greece and Turkey must have resolved their differences in the Agean Sea or have submitted the matter to the International Court for decision. The EU is not only a community of mutual prosperity, but also a community of shared risks.

LIMITS TO THE USE OF MEMBERSHIP
AS A FOREIGN POLICY INSTRUMENT

The temptation to instrumentalize membership candidacy to manage regional crises is understandable. The instrument can be effective. But it is no panacea. It works best where candidate countries already have begun fashioning economic structures similar to the EU's. The more a country already has helped itself, the more useful the concrete possibility of EU-admission is for it. On the other hand, the more distant that possibility, the less effective the instrument. In the latter case, it may prove blunt because the accession date lies too far in the future to reduce domestic and international conflicts. Then appeals for sacrifices to reduce the potential for conflict and meet EU-membership requirements may lead to undesirable political reactions.

Nevertheless, European foreign ministers appear unable to resist offering the prospect of full membership to countries, which, if at all, are decades away from accession. Their reason for doing so lies in the dearth of alternative instruments. The Union lacks effective means to achieve stability on its borders without admitting new members. One can put it differently: it yet has devised no way to bind states to the Union short of promising them full membership.

That is a strategic mistake with serious consequences. Without an instrument not involving eventual membership for associated states, the EU never can establish secure, permanent borders.

Sooner or later, the EU's leaders will have to decide just where the Community's borders lie. They also will have to develop an attractive alternative to full membership for non-members. One possibility might be to offer them all the advantages of the Common Market without allowing them to participate in the making of its laws. Instead, the Union would cooperate with them through a coordinating council.

In any event, when the EU succeeds in establishing its borders, expansion or the promise of expansion no longer will be credible as a basis for a common foreign policy. From that point onward, the EU will have to conduct foreign policy like a great power.

REFORMS

Can an EU with about 30 member countries create a credible, common foreign policy? Probably, as demanded by the former Commission President Jacques Delors, only when a group of members unite in a core Europe. Over and above that, ambition and capability to conduct not just regional, but also world foreign policy will be essential. Formation of a core Europe therefore will bring it inexorably into a relationship of rivalry with other great powers. Then, at the latest, it will become apparent that, through expansion and concentration a new, major actor in international politics will have emerged. It would be the great power Europe.

However, the need for institutional reform is urgent. Already, with just 15 member-countries, the EU's procedures and institutions are not functioning well.[28] If they remain unchanged, they will become even less effective when the Community grows to include 27 or 30 or more members.[29] Then institutional reform will become correspondingly more difficult too, conceivably leading to severe crises that could leave the Community as little more than a free trade area.[30]

Bearing these dangers in mind, the EU's enlargement likely will proceed along three axes over the next 20 to 50 years.[31] First, it will organize "Europe's" territory. Besides defining its borders, that will involve resolution of economic and trade issues, while achieving a limited level of political integration. To prevent the system's collapse, institutional reform will enjoy a high priority.[32] Within Europe's territory, member-countries will retain control over all matters not requiring common solutions or regulations.

Second, Europe must provide for a common defense. As mentioned earlier, this process is well underway. To become operational, though, a common defense requires active participation from those countries with significant military assets and capabilities. Accordingly, it is noteworthy, that Britain, France, and Germany have designated substantial troop contingents for a joint force.[33] In addition, a public mechanism for quick and effective decision-making will be necessary.

Third, the EU finally will address the integration issue. Obviously, full integration is not a realistic, near-term goal for 30 countries having very different political traditions, cultures, and levels of socioeconomic development. To attempt comprehensive integration in light of these differences likely would lead to failure. A more realistic option would be integration of those countries having the political will for it and whose socioeconomic conditions are highly similar. At the moment, that could be a constellation a small as the Community's six original members or as large as the entire Euro-zone. The latter currently includes eleven countries, to be joined by Greece in 2001. Depending on the outcome of their pending national referenda, Denmark and Sweden could join the

---

[28] The debate on drafting a written constitution for the EU and harmonizing taxation of bank accounts within the EU are cases in point. See "Herzogs Experiment: Die Wertegemeinschaft Europa im Labor: 62 Delegierte auf der Suche nach einer Grundrechtscharta", Christian Wernicke, *Die Zeit*, 16. März 2000, p. 6; and "EU Officials Fail to Get Deal on Tax", Barry James, *International Herald Tribune*, June 6, 2000, p. 1.

[29] "Before It Enlarges, Europe Must Put Its House in Order", Roy Denman, *Interntional Herald Tribune*, February 15, 2000, p. 7; and "Brüssel steht vor dem Infarkt", Christian Wernicke, *Die Zeit*, 11. Mai 2000, p. 11.

[30] "Ist die Zeit jetzt reif – für einen Wortbruch?: Europa solle erst renoviert und dann erweitert werden, hieß es immer. Doch die Reformen bleiben ein Flickwerk", Christian Wernicke, *Die Zeit*, 9. Dezember 1999, p. 6.

[31] "Building the Europe of Tomorrow", Theo Sommer, *IHJ Bulletin*, (International House of Japan), vol. 20, No. 1, Winter 2000, pp. 1-4; and "Nach den Skandalen: Was jetzt geschehen muss: Besinnung auf das Wesentliche", Helmut Schmidt, *Die Zeit*, 30. März 2000.

[32] "Vom Guten und gerechten Regieren: Die Europäische Union findet sich unversehens in einer Verfassungsdebatte wieder", Joachim Fritz-Vannahme, *Die Zeit*, 17. Februar 2000, p. 11.

[33] "...While Germany Points the Way to a Strong Self-Sufficiency", François Heisbourg, *International Herald Tribune*, May 24, 2000, p. 8.

other 12 countries within the following year. Euroland's total population then would exceed that of the United States.

Will such integration take a federative approach?[34] That would require an initiative by the founding members – France, Germany and Italy, plus Benelux – and some other willing and determined candidates. For this process to be effective, it will need additional institutions: a council, a parliamentary structure that could have operational links with the national parliaments, but probably not a Commission.[35] In effect, these bodies would be new institutions inside the EU's existing institutions.[36]

The sole constraints that the non-participating countries reasonably might impose are: (1) that this new group of core-Europeans must respect all commitments of the larger European Union; and (2) that the new institutions must not enter into conflict with those established for the whole EU. Core-Europe then could constitute a political entity on the European continent much like the United States on the North American continent.[37]

CONCLUSION

In any event, the October 1999 report to the European Commission submitted by Jean Luc Dehaene, Lord Simon, and Richard von Weizsäcker argued forcefully for greater flexibility and differentiation in the integration process. The larger the Community in their view, the more inescapable compartmentalization, like that just described, will be within it. Various states thus will move toward common goals at different speeds, attaining different levels of integration along the way. Indeed, both Schengenland (EU-members with no controls on their common borders) and Euroland (the EU-countries with a common currency) already exist as examples of such differentiated integration among the current 15 members.

Indeed, in the 1950s, members of the European Parliament were appointed, not elected, and Parliament had hardly any rights. Today, in contrast, members are chosen in general elections. Moreover, the President of the Brussels Commission and his 19 colleagues must have majority approval from Parliament. A similar, gradual development occurred in the monetary area, beginning with the currency "snake" in the early 1970s, next growing into the European Currency Union with the Ecu, and eventually evolving into the common currency, Euro. Any European, who in 1950 had proposed a European Union of fifteen countries, with all its current competencies, instead of the Schumann

---

[34] The federalist approach has skeptics in the member countries. See, "Jean-Pierre Chevènement: Der Souveränist", *Die Zeit*, 21. Juni 2000, p. 14. Some candidate countries, for example Poland, also are skeptical about a federative approach. See "Mixed Reactions in Poland to Fischer's EU Concept", n.a., *Frankfurter Allgemeine Zeitung*, (English Edition), May 16, 2000, p. 1.

[35] "Eine Föderation akzeptieren!", Jean-Louis Blanco, Sylvie Goulard, and Alfred Grosser, *Die Zeit*, 21. Juni 2000, pp. 16-17.

[36] "A Balancing Act for EU Federalists", Reginald Dale, *International Herald Tribune*, June 6, 2000, p. 11.

[37] "Federal Europe: Hardly a Radical Plan", Reginald Dale, *International Herald Tribune*, May 23, 2000, p. 13.

Plan for a Coal and Steel Community with just six countries, would not have been taken seriously.

Despite all its defects, the European Union at its present stage of development is in many respects a great success. It would have been unimaginable for Bismarck or Poincaré, for Wilhelm II absurd and undesirable, even for Briand and Stresemann today's EU would have been at most a distant dream.[38] Neither Schumann nor Adenauer nor de Gaulle thought so far into the future. The Atlantic Alliance maintained peace in Europe for forty years in face of the Soviet threat. However, peace among countries on that part of the Continent that was free of Soviet domination resulted from the first steps toward European integration. Neither for the Italians nor the Finns, the Spaniards or the Austrians, the French or the Germans has there ever before been such a long period of peace, coupled with the expectation that it would continue indefinitely into the future.

The history of European integration therefore is a story of gradual development. This development repeatedly has experienced crises and setbacks. In fact, the first crisis came in 1954, just a few years after the ECSC's founding, when the French Parliament rejected the European Defense Union Treaty. But Paris and Bonn overcame that crisis, and all the successive ones as well, in order to keep making progress toward a united Europe.[39] Hence, the future likely will see a continuation of present policies: gradual reform of the European Union's institutions, gradual expansion of its responsibilities, and gradual accession of additional member-countries.

---

[38]"Außenpolitik im Widerspruch: Was Gustav Stresemann erreichte, woran er scheiterte und was daraus gelernt wurde", Joschka Fischer, *Die Zeit*, 3. Februar 2000, p. 45.; and "Europa von oben: Warum die politischen Initiativen für eine Europäische Union nach dem Ersten Weltkrieg scheiterten", Oliver Bugard, *Die Zeit*, 13. Januar 2000, p. 82.

[39] "Gute Nachbarn: Zwischen Deutschland und Frankreich steht alles zum Besten", Dominique Moisi, *Die Zeit*, 9. Dezember 1999, p. 8.

Chapter 2

€140 BILLION OUT OF THIN AIR: EUROPE'S UMTS-AUCTIONS

Robert C. Rickards
The International University in Germany
Bruchsal, Germany
and
Harz University of Applied Sciences
Wernigerode, Germany

ABSTRACT

Western Europe and Japan have developed a promising new mobile telephone technology. In 2000, many European countries held auctions for licenses permitting its use. Auction "winners", though, well may turn out to be "losers" due to high costs associated with obtaining licenses and building networks. In addition, the extent of future customer acceptance and willingness to pay remain highly uncertain. Consequently, Europe's major telecommunications firms already find themselves in financial difficulties. These difficulties have had serious negative effects on the latest European license auctions. Nevertheless, the European and Japanese telecommunications indurtries enjoy a considerable lead over their American rival in the race to exploit this new technology commercially.

INTRODUCTION

When dry acronymns like "3G" and "UMTS" appear in the evening news, then likely either lots of money, or extraordinary secretiveness, or incalculable opportunities and risks are at stake. In this case, all are involved.[1] The cryptic expressions refer to the third-generation Universal Mobile Telecommunications System. This system represents a new

---

[1] Lütge, Gunhild, "Pokern um die Zukunft," *Die Zeit*, 3. August 2000, p. 1.

mobile telephone technology, predicted by many analysts to have a bright future. Yet as promising as its future may be, the system alone hardly could have caused the furor that occurred in Europe in 2000. Instead, it was the more than €140 billion ($117.80 billion) paid by telecommunications companies for the licenses necessary to exploit UMTS-technology that excited everyone's imagination. In succession, the governments of the United Kingdom, the Netherlands, Germany, and Italy auctioned these licenses to the highest bidder. Essentially, a series of widely publicized, very high stakes poker games resulted, the largest of which took place in Germany, Europe's richest telecommunications market.

This article begins with a brief discussion of various designs for such auctions and a frequently observed outcome, the "winner's curse". Next, it describes Germany's radio frequencies, their regulation, and the German UMTS-auction, together with its winners and losers. The article then examines the French license distribution process as an alternative to public auctions. It goes on to analyze the new business field involved as well as the growing skepticism about its profitability and employment effects. Returning to the topic of the winner's curse, the article reports the difficulties now confronting French, German, and other European telecommunications firms. After analyzing the German auction's consequences for neighboring, particularly East European, countries, it reports on both the Italian and Swiss auction fiascos. Finally, the article closes with a few thoughts about the current radio frequency situation in the United States.

THE "ENGLISH SIMULTANEOUS" AUCTION

Some wags have suggested that the British, Dutch, German, and Italian governments just wanted to raise as much cash as possible. Indeed, as discussed below, various European countries used other methods to distribute their UMTS-licenses. But while the sale's huge proceeds no doubt pleased Hans Eichel, the German Finance Minister, an auction probably was the best vehicle for transferring a scarce, public good to the private sector.

Indeed, the United States has been using auctions for some time to sell oil exploitation rights and electricity as well as to award street construction contracts and air pollution quotas. Mexico is planning to do the same in privatizing its rail network and the state-owned gold, silver, and phosphate mines. Auctions are the preferred vehicles for these ownership transfers because they supposedly are fairer and more transparent than the classic public bidding process, which is much more susceptible to cronyism. Nevertheless, business researchers warn against organizing this kind of sale without an auction designer's expert advice. Because Berlin went ahead without first obtaining their advice, auction designers criticized Germany's rules in advance of the sale as complicated, inimicable to competition, and unlikely to maximize the government's proceeds.

The German rules foresaw a so-called "English simultaneous" auction. "English" because, just as at Sotheby's in London, the participants must overbid each other.

"Simultaneous", because 12 radio frequency packages were offered for bids at the same time. Thus, it was as if Sotheby's would auction twelve identical stamps at once. In the end, whoever had bid the most for two frequency packages would receive a "small" mobile communications license. The highest bidder for three packages would receive a "large" one with correspondingly greater data transmission capacity. Thus, whether four "large", six "small", or a combination of "small" and "large" licenses actually had been put up for sale would not be clear until the end of the auction. That certainly was confusing.

Some observers prophecied that the four established mobile telephone operators in Germany (Mannesmann Mobilfunk, T-Mobil, E-Plus and Viag Interkom) each would acquire a "large" license. These four firms had a competitive advantage due to their investments in the existing mobile communications network and their customer bases. They therefore could be expected to bid high enough to shut out financially weaker, prospective market entrants. Theoretically two newcomers were possible, but critics said in practice the auction's rules would lead to cementing the status quo.

That necessarily would have been bad for competition. Precisely for this reason, London reserved one of the licenses it auctioned for a new market entrant. For its part, Berlin wanted at least one new firm to enter the German UMTS-market too. But the risk of provoking a legal battle by showing such preference for one competitor proved to be greater than the German government was willing to accept.

OTHER AUCTION DESIGNS

To understand the critics' objections, it may be helpful first to consider several other auction forms and their outcomes. For example, take a Sotheby's auction and compare it to a flower auction in Amsterdam. In the tulip trade, speed is essential, because compared to Old Masters flowers have a very short shelflife. A Dutch auctioneer therefore calls a plausible highest bid out into the hall and lowers the price until a participant accepts the last mentioned amount. In this way, good traders auction off their flower lots in a rhythm of several seconds and realize the highest prices anyone is willing to pay. Auction designers call these "sinking" auctions a "Dutch Auction" or a "Holland Auction".

Next, turn to the case of New Zealand, the first country to auction mobile communications and television licenses. It chose an even more curious design, the "secret, second-place auction". According to its rules, every bidder turns in an offer in a closed envelope. The bidder with the highest offer wins, but pays only the price of the second highest bid. Auction designers have calculated that this form of auction approximates the same result as the English auction. After all, at Sotheby's a painting will not be sold for the highest price that the winner ultimately would have been prepared to pay. Instead, it goes for an amount just above the pain threshold of the second highest bidder.

In practice, though, New Zealand's secret, second-place auction produced some grotesque outcomes. In one case, a firm had bid NZ$100,000, but then got the license for the second highest offer of just NZ$6. Another time, the highest offer was NZ$7 million, while the price paid was merely NZ$5,000. A student at Otaga University even received a license for a small city for free. He had bid only NZ$1. Since there was no second bidder, though, he won the auction and paid the price of the second offer, namely nothing. Because often there were few participants, auction designers said the New Zealand government should have had a rule establishing minimum bids.

In its 1995 auction of 99 spectrum licenses for mobile telephones, portable fax machines, and cordless computer nets, the U.S. government included many interesting details in the bidding rules. Among others, its auction designers were able to take into account a requirement that some of those licenses go to firms headed by women or minority group members. The auction rules foresaw that while these firms could engage in normal bidding for certain licenses, in the end they need not pay the full amount of their bids. The preferred groups thereby got a ten-percent discount and also received ten percent more licenses than they otherwise would have.

For auction designers, the successful sale of mobile communication licenses marks a triumph of game theory. From their perspective, an auction is just a game with special, clearly defined rules. In order to evaluate different auction designs, game theorists analyze how rules, strategy, and results affect each other, underpinning their analyses with computer simulations and test auctions. As the great spectrum auction in the United States approached, every larger telephone company therefore hired consultants familiar with game theory. In contrast, the German regulatory authority proved "consultant resistant". Critics asserted that it had paid too little attention to various aspects of the sale's design. Consequently, confusion, exclusion of new entrants from the market, and suboptimal auction proceeds would result.[2]

THE WINNER'S CURSE

Suboptimal auction proceeds, however, need not mean low revenues. On the contrary, scientific tests employing students as subjects have demonstrated how a phenomenon researchers call the "winner's curse" works. Suppose you want a little pocket money to finance a visit to the neighborhood tavern. You fill a glass jar with about eight dollars in coins and auction it off among the tavern's guests. *On average*, they will underestimate the value of the jar's contents, guessing that it holds only five dollars in coins. Nevertheless, there almost always are some *individuals*, who overestimate the contents' value and bid too high, ten dollars or more, for the jar. Such auctions are "won" by the persons, who overbid the most and consequently realize the greatest loss.

The winner's curse phenomenon has been observed in the case of oil firms competing for production rights in Mexico. Whichever company most overestimated an oil field's production potential bid the most and won those rights. The resulting profits were lower than the interest a bank would have paid on the same amount of money deposited in a

---

[2] Rauner, Max, "Die Mathematik des Auktionators", *Die Zeit*, 27. Juli 2000, p.32.

savings account! In fact, Texaco paid seven times more than would have been reasonable for its Mexican oil fields.[3]

Apparently, even intelligent people have difficulty seeing through this sort of game. Thus, governments are tempted to play it again and again. The UMTS-license auctions are a good case in point. In effect, the authorities simply offered some licenses, sequestered the international telephone companies' representatives incommunicado somewhere, waited, and hoped. While auction designers wrinkled their brows and stockholders wrung their hands, some top corporate decisionmakers continued raising their bids beyond the amount of any likely return on their investment.

At the British auction, five bidders offered the grand sum of $36 billion for the new mobile telephone frequencies, a staggering price that dumbfounded most commentators. Analysts worried that the winners had paid too much to tap into unproven commercial possibilities. But this auction and its successors were key elements in the business strategies of some of the world's largest telecommunciations firms. For European operators, the auctions constituted an opportunity to consolidate their technological lead in wireless data services over the United States and to challenge American domination of the Internet. To attain the necessary economies of scale, however, they would have to build pan-European networks. That, in turn, necessitated obtaining UMTS-licenses in every major European market, starting with the United Kingdom.

For the (un-)lucky bidders, the gigantic expenditures this strategy involved promised to be a ball and chain around their legs for years to come. Nonetheless, they believed it better to enter the auspicious-looking market for 3G-mobile telephony with an impediment than to be absent from it altogether. So, whether they liked it or not, the established mobile telephone companies had to participate in the auction because without additional frequencies they ultimately would fail in this new business field.

GERMAN FREQUENCIES AND FREQUENCY REGULATIONS

At present, the "Administrative Principles of the Regulatory Authority for Telecommunications and Mail Pertaining to the Division of Frequency Ranges into Individual Frequency Uses As Well As to the Determination of These Frequency Uses", the "Administrative Principles for Frequency Usage" in short, or shorter still the "VwGrds-FreqN" govern the issuance of German broadcasting and telecommunications licenses. This monumental work of German regulatory law weighs two-and-one-half kilograms (5.63 lbs.). Even so, it still represents only the provisional last word on the subject. Hence, the German government continues to urge manufacturers or importers of cellular telephones and such to obtain additional regulatory clarification before bringing new appliances onto the market (umts.regtp.de).[4]

---

[3] Paulus, Jochen, "Fluch der Gewinner", *Die Zeit*, 24. August 2000, p. 21.

[4] Albrecht, Jörg, "Warten auf den Babelfisch: Eine Behörde kämpft mit dem Wellensalat im Äther," *Die Zeit*, 17. August 2000, p. 27.

That is because there already is a lot of broadcasting in Germany, starting with five kilohertz (low frequency induction facilities for transmission of speech and music in movie theaters, churches and theaters) across 419.72 megahertz (countrywide data broadcasting exclusively for operating railyard locomotives via remote control) to 252 gigahertz (passive sensors onboard satellites for mapping the earth's properties). Unfortunately, the VwGrds-FreqN has not caused Mannesmann Mobilfunk to lie down peacefully beside T-Mobil like the Biblical lion alongside the lamb. Instead, a free-for-all has been underway to obtain more frequencies for new uses.

Thus, the regulatory agency has felt obliged to improve upon the VwGrds-FreqN. To that end, it has created supplementary "Rules for the Conduct of the Auction Process for the Awarding of Licenses for UMTS" under the file number BK-1b-98/005-2. On 34 cleanly printed pages, ordered from A to E, these rules are in their verbiage at best comparable only with the work of Holderlin, when he was on the verge of complete insanity. Consequently, all UMTS-auction participants had to undergo special schooling in the process rules prior to beginning of the sale.

GERMANY'S UMTS-AUCTION

After the unexpectedly high bidding in the U.K., telecommunications companies apparently became warier. At its auction, the Dutch government managed to raise just one-third of the amount it had expected.[5] The resultant uncertainty about the sale's outcome, together with the unusual circumstances in which it was to take place, heightened the suspense surrounding Germany's UMTS-auction. The radio frequencies indeed were not auctioned like Old Masters. Secretive civil servants disappeared onto the former U.S. military base at Mainz-Gonsenheim, which was equipped with rooms and telephones secured against electronic eavesdropping. The whole circus was justified with the argument that licenseholders would have the right to transmit voices, images, moving images and data throughout Germany for the next 20 years.

Although initially thirteen groups indicated interest, in the end there were just seven bidders in the German auction. Four of the latter were incumbent operators of the current generation of mobile telephone networks. They are: Deutsche Telekom AG; the Mannesmann Mobilfunk operations of Britain's Vodafone AirTouch PLC; VIAG Interkom together with its major shareholder, British Telecommunications PLC; the E-Plus service operated by Hutchison Whampoa Ltd. of Hong Kong; and KPN NV of the Netherlands. Other bidders included MobilCom, in which France Télécom SA has a big stake; Debitel, which is backed by SwissCom AG, and a consortium including Sonera Corp. of Finland and Teléfonica SA of Spain.

Klaus-Dieter Scheurle, president of the German regulatory authority for telecommunications and postal services, personally greeted the seven applicants' representatives and the many observers. After the ruling coalition of Social Democrats

---

[5] Schmid, John, "Low Bids Mark Auction of Cell Phone Licenses," *International Herald Tribune*, August 1, 2000, p. 11.

(SPD) and Greens took power in Berlin in 1998, most commentators thought it a foregone conclusion that Scheurle would be replaced. In late 1997, when the Postal Ministry was broken up, Scheurle's appointment as head of the new authority caused serious disagreement among the political parties. The opposition Christian Democratic Union and the SPD each had wanted to appoint a member of their own party. On taking office, the 43-year-old Scheurle (a member of the Christian Social Union, CSU) already had a meteoric career behind him, the kind that only is possible as a serving minister's protégé. In this case, Scheurle's political godfather was the CSU's Postal Minister, Wolfgang Bötsch. Convinced of Scheurle's qualities, Bötsch boxed his appointment through.[6] It was Scheurle, who then built up the telecommunications and postal regulatory authority and planned Germany's auction as a new source of government revenue.[7]

Scheurle explained the bidding rules to the participants. The auction began, though, only after a 90-minute delay. The seven mobile operators' representatives apparently had to deal with some technical hitches first. That included the installation of bug-proof lines to their corporate headquarters to prevent their competitors listening in on them. For the auction's duration, these representatives also had to remain isolated from one another and the outside world in small, hermetically sealed offices. They communicated with the auctioneer via computer.

MobilCom surprised its rivals by bidding more than DM1 billion for two blocks of frequencies in the first round. Mindful of the lavish U.K. prices and the more realistic Dutch ones, the other six auction participants cautiously limited themselves to the minimum bid of DM100 million per frequency range set by the government telecommunications regulatory agency. Total offers in the first round thus reached about DM1.65 billion.

In the second round, the bid total rose to around DM2.15 billion. Industry leaders Mannesmann and Deutsche Telekom revealed their bidding strategy for the first time by making the highest offers for three frequency ranges, which they would need for large numbers of customers. Debitel still held back at this point, but the complicated rules governing the auction forced it to the fore in round three with the highest bid.

In rounds four and five, the bids increased no more than the 10 percent minimum raise over the previous high that was decreed by the regulatory authority. By the end of the auction's first day, the bid total was DM2.28 billion for the 12 available frequency ranges. Mannesmann and Viag Interkom put in the highest bids for three frequency ranges each, while Deutsche Telekom and MobilCom were high bidders on two bundles

---

[6] Stüwe, Heinz, "The Real Auctioneer," *Frankfurter Allgemeine Zeitung*, (English Edition), August 1, 2000, p. 2.

[7] After three years as the president of Germany's telecommunications and post regulatory authority, Mr. Scheurle seems to have grown weary of the continuous political disputes. He will leave his office at the end of 2000. N.a., "Scheurle Resigns from His Post," *Frankfurter Allgemeine Zeitung*, (English Edition), November 24, 2000, p. 5.

apiece. E-Plus and Debitel were high bidders on one each, while the consortium made up of Spain's Teléfonica and the Finnish company Sonera had no highest bids.[8]

As subsequent events proved, though, prices still had plenty of time to rise. The auction continued for three more weeks. As it progressed, the sums bid rose, sometimes in tiny increments, other times by large amounts. Both the highest bidding firm and the number of licenses likely to be sold changed frequently. Ultimately, though, the six winning bidders each received a "small" license. Together, these firms paid the princely sum of DM98.8 billion ($50.5 billion)!

WINNERS AND LOSERS

The clear winner in the auction was the German federal government. It plans to spend its huge windfall entirely on debt retirement. The German state governments, however, came away empty-handed. That led Kurt Faltlhauser, Finance Minister of the state of Bavaria, to threaten the federal government with a suit before Germany's highest court, if the states did not get their share of the license proceeds. Faltlhauser argued that those mobile telecommunications companies, which bought licenses, could write off the cost against their income, thereby substantially reducing the companies' state and municipal tax liabilities. Without some form of compensation from the federal government, the states and municipalities would suffer substantial revenue losses due to Berlin's good fortune.[9] By enacting Eichel's proposed budget for 2001, the German Bundestag ultimately rejected Faltlhauser's argument.

Not only Eichel can be happy about the 3G UMTS-license auction's outcome. Indirectly, investors buying German federal government paper also can profit from it. The reason is the Finance Minister's fiscal policy. Because the Bundestag approved earmarking the auction receipts exclusively for debt reduction, the federal government will make less use of deficit financing in 2001. Ceteris paribus, a reduced supply of debt ought to cause the price of government bonds to rise. Anticipating this development, prices for paper maturing in five to ten years already have risen.

But the market for corporate bonds should prove even more interesting. After all, the "cursed winners", the telephone companies, now have to raise the gigantic sums they bid for the UMTS-licenses. For example, British Telecom recently has announced that it will market around $10 billion of such bonds with a fixed duration and interest. The Finnish telephone company, Sonera, supposedly is planning an issue of around €5 billion. In addition, France Télécom has toyed with the notion of borrowing €7 billion or more from investors. Meanwhile other countries, including Austria, Belgium, and Italy have auctioned licenses too. Consequently, experts anticipate the telecommunication companies will float a veritable flood of loans in 2001. Altogether, these firms could

---

[8] N.a., "UMTS-Auction Bidders Dig In for Long Haul," Frankfurter Allgemeine Zeitung, (English Edition), August 1, 2000, p.1.

[9] N.a., "Bavaria Wants a Share in UMTS Billions", Frankfurter Allgemeine Zeitung, (English Edition), September 6, 2000, p. 1.

issue bonds in a volume up to DM65 billion ($33.2 billion). In order to attract investors to particular issues within this large, overall bond sale, the telecommunication concerns will have to offer really generous coupon rates.[10]

AN ALTERNATIVE LICENSE DISTRIBUTION PROCESS

France's Finance Minister Laurent Fabius shows no regret. His country (along with Scandinavia and Spain) decided against an auction to distribute its UMTS-licenses. Instead, France has made four, fifteen-year UMTS-licenses available for a bargain price. Paris will lease the sought-after frequencies for DM9.7 billion ($5 billion) each. That means, Fabius will be taking in only about DM38.8 billion ($19.8 billion), less than half the revenues of his German colleague, Eichel.

Fabius's timing hardly could have been worse. France's distribution procedure began just as everyone was congratulating the German Finance Minister on all the unexpected revenue the Mainz auction had produced. Citizens' action groups immediately criticized the French government for the big present it plans to give the telecommunications firms. The action groups said both that the price for the leases was too low and that the method of payment was highly favorable to the phone companies. Although the latter must pay half the license amount during the lease's first two years, the balance will not be due until 2016. The French telecommunication concerns France Télécom, Cegetel, and Bouygues nevertheless unanimously had complained that the government's price was too high. Indeed, the country's third largest mobile communications firm, Bouygues, lodged an anticompetitiveness complaint with the European Union in Brussels. The French companies muted their outcry, though, once the German auction began producing high bids.

In contrast to the situation in Germany, the French licenses will be awarded in a sort of beauty contest to whomever presents the government with a sufficiently convincing case. The role of the jury will be played by a formally independent regulatory agency. Using 14 criteria, it can award an applicant up to five hundred points. The criteria emphasize an optimal service distribution across the country, the credibility of the applicant's business plan, and the volume of multimedia services offered. New jobs and protection of the environment during the network's construction are relatively less important criteria. Although domestic critics have complained that the proposed criteria are too unspecific, the government has set an application deadline at the beginning of 2001. A decision on the awards will be forthcoming in 2002.

Experts think it likely that the French compeititors France Télécom, Cegetel, and Bouygues will receive licenses. All the suspense therefore is concentrated on the awarding of the fourth license. About ten other applicants are competing for it. Much to the chagrin of foreign companies, a fourth French firm, Suez Lyonnaise des Eaux, probably has the best prospects of obtaining this license. The Lyonnaise has formed a

---

[10] Brost, Marc, "Vom UMTS-Geld profitieren auch die Anleger", *Die Zeit*, 24. August, 2000, p.24.

consortium with the Spanish Telefónica, which remains open to additional partners. Nevertheless, there has been considerable protest from abroad because it appears France intends to give its industry preference by discriminating against foreign competitors.

The different license distribution practices throughout Europe are particularly annoying to Ron Sommer, Deutsche Telekom's CEO. He regards an auction as the fairest distribution method because it avoids distorting competition in other countries. For example, France Télécom found itself in a particularly good situation to participate in the German license bidding after the French government decided against an auction of its own. The French joined forces with Telekom's main domestic rival MobilCom. The money saved in France, thus became available to the France Télécom-MobilCom consortium for raising bids at Germany's auction. (The same is true for Finland, Sweden, Norway, and Spain, which distributed free licenses to their domestic telephone companies.) France Télécom especially welcomed the French government's decision because it already had exhausted itself financially in the British auction with its partner Orange. Still France Télécom's majority shareholder, the French government obviously has a vested interest in the concern's welfare too.

For his part, Sommer must fear that, just as in Spain, Deutsche Telekom will get no licenses in France. Since his concern fell out with France Télécom, it has been represented in the bordering country only through the telephone firm Siris, which specializes in business customers, and the Internet provider Club-Internet. Hence, an entry into the French mobile communications market has the highest priority for him.

Efforts to convince the profit-oriented businessman and Club-Internet boss Jean-Luc Lagardère to make common cause in the UMTS-license distribution have failed however. Yet an alliance with a domestic candidate is the sole way for Sommer still to enter the French mobile communications business. The Bouygues-Group has confirmed it would be prepared to give the Germans a minority interest in an alliance with a foreign partner. But the Group also intends to open talks with other foreign competitors like the Dutch KPN and the Japanese NTT DoCoMo.[11]

THE PRIZE

The object of all this corporate and governmental wheeling and dealing is a prize of unknown value. Although the Old Continent practically slept through the first phases of the Internet revolution, in the case of mobile telecommunications it has been Johnny-on-the-spot. In fact, as shown in Table 1, mobile telecommunications is one high-tech market, in which Europe is preeminent.

The worldwide success of the European second-generation, GMS-standard for cellular handsets shocked most U.S. telecommunications companies. At present, 350 million people telephone with this technology. In the first half of 2000 alone, the number of GSM-users increased 22%. Just here in Germany, there already are some 30 million

---

[11] Kläsgen, Michael, "Ausländer raus? Paris vergibt die Lizenzen nach Gusto – ein umstrittenes Verfahren", *Die Zeit*, 24. August, 2000, p. 21.

mobile phones in use. With no let-up in sales in sight, that number well could increase to 50 million by year's end.[12] Mobile telecommunications thus represent a field in which globalization is not a one-way street. European companies are betting that the cellular telephone boom will continue. Deutsche Telekom's recent purchase of an American mobile telecommunications company, Voicestream, is further evidence of their confidence.

Table 1: Mobile Telephone Market Share 1999

Provider	Market Share (Worldwide in Percent)
Nokia	26.9
Motorola	16.9
Ericsson	10.5
Samsung	6.2
Panasonic	5.5
Siemens	4.6
Alcatel	4.1
Mitsubishi (Trium)	3.4
Phillips	3.3
NEC	3.2
QUALCOMM	2.6
SAGEM	2.4
Toshiba	2.1
Others	8.4

Of course the Europeans' current lead may not last. Europe has a history of pioneering developments, then squandering its lead. Urgent action is necessary to tackle information-technology skill shortages and the lack of entrepreneurship if that is not to happen again. The Europeans want to combine their entirely new, 3G UMTS-technology with an American invention, the Internet. The two technologies complement one another nicely. UMTS delivers a data superhighway via high-speed, digital handset (handy), while the Internet's worldwide web offers new options for supplying tailored information and attractive services. The cellular handsets of the near future, therefore, will combine all the functions of a traditional mobile phone with all the capabilities of a pocket computer. Instead of a mini-screen, they will have much larger, color displays as well as a small keyboard or voice recognition system. In addition, these new machines will have microphones, cameras and scanners and will be able both to send and receive transmissions with impeccable quality.

Mobile video conferences, in which participants can see each other on their handy screens, also will be possible once built-in cameras have become standard. In other

---

[12] Schmidt, Holger, "Government Heralds Dawn of New Telecoms Era," *Frankfurter Allgemeine Zeitung*, (English Edition), August 1, 2000, pp.1-2.

words, this new generation of cellular phones will give professional users a pocket-sized, mobile office. Other services handys will provide include: playing music, showing films, reporting stock market prices, engaging in e-commerce, receiving and sending e-mails, ordering and paying for tickets, and transferring money.[13] They will allow remote control of the heating in stationary cars and show motorists the quickest way out of traffic jams. In Scandinavia, beverage vending machines already spit out cola cans when they receive the appropriate handy signal. At the same time, the cost is deducted automatically from the customer's bank account.

At least initially, the new UMTS-phones will be significantly more expensive than today's models. Yet if competition proves as tough as it is expected to be, prices soon will plummet. Billing methods will have to be adapted to the new technology too. Because data henceforth will be transmitted in packages, much as they are on the Internet, it no longer will be transmission time, but rather data volume which determines cost. Users thus will be able to have permanent connections without running up enormous telephone bills.

In order to have a chance of succeeding on the requisite large scale, however, European telecommunications companies first had to obtain licenses in at least several major markets. Having done so, they next must invest additional billions to construct new mobile phone networks and distill from the Internet's infinite possibilities an attractive assortment of new services. Only then will they discover whether the wonderful, but expensive 3G UMTS-technology can acquire a mass market. Until customers finally begin to pay, the prudence of the mind-boggling prices the telecommunications giants paid for a piece of the airwaves will remain questionable.

Today, most UMTS-licensees do not have a solid business plan for recovering the high expenditures for a license and subsequent network construction. In addition, charges for mobile calls soon will be on a flat-rate basis and not per minute. For both reasons, network operators have become more oriented toward partnerships with content providers.

One such potential partner is Bertelsmann e-Commerce Group. It is a subsidiary of German media giant Bertelsmann and plans to enter the cellular-telephone market as a "virtual network" operator. Accordingly, it currently is in negotiations with all companies that have acquired a 3G UMTS mobile-telephone license in Germany with the exception of Vodafone-Mannesmann. Industry insiders view Deutsche Telekom as the partner of choice because it also could offer access to the U.S. market through Voicestream. Sources have said a final decision on a network partner will come early in 2001.[14]

A virtual network operator buys cellular-telephone capacities from an actual UMTS-network operator in order to sell them under its own name and on its own account. Bertelsmann thus does not want to be merely a portal operator for UMTS-telephones.

---

[13] For an overview of the most important e-business applications of Internet- and UMTS-technologies, see Palme, Klaus, "eBusiness: Neue Aufgaben für den Controller-Dienst", *Der Controlling Berater*, Heft 6, 17. November 2000, pp. 15-42.

[14] Schmid, Holger, "Bertelsmann to Make Waves in Mobile-Phone Market," *Frankfurter Allgemeine Zeitung*, (English Edition), November 28, 2000, p. 5.

Instead, it intends to create true customer relationships via UMTS-mobile telephony in order to sell its own media offerings.

Music well may be the most important entertainment offering for cell phones in the future. Music lovers then will not have to save songs because data transfer soon will be so fast and cheap that they will be able to download and listen to music at the same time. The music will come either from a central computer or from the computer of another member of a collectors club, which could operate in a fashion similar to today's 42-million-member-strong Napster.

The exchange of data among Internet users originated by Napster likely will affect other content markets such as the film industry and the book branch too. Bertelsmann currently is negotiating with film studios to develop similar data-sharing models. Such developments will have to wait though, because the bandwidth for the data transfer is not yet available.

Bertelsmann e-Commerce Group is a part of the newly created Direct Group, which also includes Bertelsmann-owned book clubs in 24 countries. Bertelsmann e-Commerce Group comprises 16 Internet businesses, among them the online book retailers BOL and barnesandnoble.com, as well as Internet music retailer CDNow.

GROWING SKEPTICISM ABOUT PROFITABILITY

In the meantime, plenty still can go wrong. Together, the European mobile network operators are investing hundreds of billions of dollars without any reliable information about consumers' acceptance of UMTS-technology. Even now, though, it is virtually certain that the vigorous competition in this new business field will lead to a continuous downward spiral in the price of future services. Accordingly, profit margins have begun to shrink, the value of the operators' stock to fall, and strong pressures for consolidation to emerge. Many of the firms entering the UMTS-market therefore eventually either will have to abandon it or will fall victim to a corporate takeover.

In order to discover what private and business customers might be willing to pay for the new technology, researchers at Ericsson Consulting GmbH carried out a year-long study. They analyzed trends in existing mobile telecommunications services like i-mode in Japan as well as SMS and WAP in Germany. They also discussed needs and expectations with groups of private and business users. What emerged was a very rough estimate of the sums that users might be prepared to pay for UMTS-services.

As reported in Table 2, the Ericsson consultants predicted that by 2005 Germany alone will have 9.2 million UMTS-customers. By 2007, the number should rise to 17.6 million, and by 2010 to almost 35 million. The research team also found that, in contrast to GMS, business customers unlikely will seek quick access to the new technology. Instead, as early as 2002, 60% and thus the majority of UMTS-users will be normal consumers.

Table 2: Projected Numbers of UMTS-Users in Germany

Year	Number of Users (Millions)
2002	759
2003	3.287
2004	6.391
2005	9.213
2006	13.595
2007	17.696
2008	22.576
2009	28.162
2010	34.719
2011	43.326

They are prepared to pay a base charge of DM25 per month and an additional DM0.40 per minute for a conversation. Besides that, each month they want to transmit a large amount of text, eight pictures and a chart. They have little interest in downloading music, but would send 42 e-mails and use the Internet 17 times. These services would be worth DM33 and any others DM10 more to them. Together with the base and voice calling charges, that implies a monthly bill of DM100 for a private customer. Business customers would be willing to pay up to 160 DM per month.

That sounds promising. But one must interpret the numbers carefully. The Ericsson research team itself emphasizes that at present it remains quite difficult to predict realistic prices. Thus, depending on how quickly the number of customers actually grows, network operators almost certainly will face horrendous initial losses. Just putting a dense network of receiving and transmittal stations in place across Europe will swallow numerous billions. Due to a dearth of more appropriate locations in densely populated areas, skyscrapers already are being equipped with signal equipment. The battle for space on the "right" roof has been joined.

Network equipment suppliers like Alcatel, Ericsson, Nokia, Psion, and Siemens meanwhile have been contacted by everyone. Hence, they are sure of full order books. That may sound somewhat paradox. But precisely because of the high investment costs, telephone companies must expand their new infrastructure rapidly in order to get paying customers into the network as quickly as possible. In addition, they must meet various government demands. For example, the German federal government requires its auction winners to be able to supply 50% of the population by 2005.

Skepticism is growing about whether such a rapid expansion program is feasible. Supposedly, UMTS will start in 2002 not only in Germany, but also everywhere else in Europe. To meet that goal, 60 networks must be built simultaneously all over the Old Continent. By way of comparison, in years past an average of just five GMS-networks were under construction in Europe at any one time. Therefore, costly delays undoubtedly will occur. Yet despite such obstacles, the Europeans and the Japanese have a great advantage vis-a-vis the United States. After a long dispute, they have agreed on technical standards for the third generation of mobile telephones.[15] So even if instead of the hoped-for single, worldwide uniform standard, only a related technology family emerges, the way to a mass market in Europe and Asia is wide open.

GROWING SKEPTICISM ABOUT EMPLOYMENT EFFECTS

Accordingly, both the German Economics Minister, Werner Müller, and Germany's electronics industry reckon with 700,000 new, UMTS-related jobs over the next five years.[16] That sounds almost as though the government had implemented a huge employment program instead of merely raking in almost DM100.000.000.000 in auction proceeds. As just explained, the telephone companies still have to invest further billions in the construction of their networks -- without knowing whether and when the new technology will be profitable. After the bloodletting at the Mainz auction, concern bosses have been calculating their costs very carefully. That means restricting new investments in staff and equipment, while getting as much as possible out of existing capacities.

Unquestionably, the network outfitters face a rosy future. But they probably will not hire new workers on a large scale either. Precisely because the construction of network infrastructure requires only a temporary, short-term expansion of production, it is unlikely to lead to any long-run gains in permanent employment.

Left as potential new employers are those firms that plan to deliver new services via handy. How many jobs they will create, though, depends entirely on whether their visions ultimately become realities. Because there is no reliable prognosis about that either, no one ought to take the juggling with impressive employment numbers by governments and corporations seriously.

FRENCH CONCERN IN DIFFICULTY

As European phone companies grapple with mountains of debt and falling stock valuations, France Télécom SA is scaling back expectations for a sale of shares in its mobile phone unit, Orange PLC, planned for early 2001. Initially, France Télécom had planned to raise about €14 billion ($11.9 billion) by selling around 15 percent of Orange, which it bought for $36 billion this year from Vodafone Group PLC, the world's biggest mobile-phone operator. Vodafone sold Orange after acquiring it in a hostile takeover of Mannesmann AG of Germany. In November, however, France Télécom executives said

---

[15] Lester Thurow regards the European Union's ability to work out common standards among member countries as a comparative advantage relative to the United States. See his chapter in Gibson, Rowan (Hrsg.): *Rethinking the Future*, (German translation, Landsberg/Lech, 1997).

[16] Lütge, Gunhild, "Eine Luftnummer: Sämtliche Jobprognosen für UMTS sind unseriös," *Die Zeit*, 24. August 2000, p. 17.

that the initial public offering would aim to raise only between €7 billion and €10 billion.[17]

France Télécom initially had said it would sell Orange shares in London, Paris and New York. Subsequently, however, the firm chose Paris for its primary listing, with a parallel listing in London. France Télécom would have incurred a heavy tax bill had it made London its principle listing. The initial public offering is set for January and February 2001, but that could change if market conditions are unsatisfactory.

France Télécom had spent about $50 billion in 2000 to acquire both Orange and the licenses for third-generation mobile phones in various countries. The company now wants to offset some of that spending with revenues from the planned share sale. Specifically, France Télécom is seeking to raise money to buy back about $12 billion of its own stock used in the takeover of Orange from Vodafone. Furthermore, France Télécom intends to regroup all its European mobile businesses under the Orange name, which according to analysts has become a powerful brand.

But, like other European phone companies, France Télécom's plans have been frustrated at least partly by growing wariness among investors about the phone companies' debts. Moreover, the probable success of mobile Internet use has been questioned by one of its pioneers, NTT DoCoMo Inc. of Japan. A firm spokesman recently said so-called third-generation wireless devices might not prove to be money-earners. Specifically, the new technology may not be capable of downloading big Internet files of music or video clips likely to be one of the device's attractions for youthful customers.

France Télécom's announcements have reminded investors of the European phone firms' indebtedness. Stock prices have fallen anew. Particularly hard hit have been France Télécom and British Telecommunications PLC, which also plans a major restructuring to cut some $14.5 billion off its debts.

As stock prices have fallen, European companies have found it increasingly difficult to raise money on equity markets. When Teléfonica SA of Spain sold shares in its wireless subsidiary in November 2000, it earned €3.3 billion, roughly half the amount forecast six months earlier. In the Netherlands, KPN NV postponed a flotation of its mobile business until sometime in 2001. With debt approaching $17.85 billion, KPN's shares have fallen by 64 percent this year.

The looming prospect of numerous initial public offerings likely to be floated in 2001 is depressing current stock prices even more. Besides Orange, KPN, and T-Mobil, a Deutsche Telekom AG unit, the mobile arms of most national operators are planning share sales to recover from debt. While investors thus will have a chance to pick among them, the telecommunication concerns will find themselves in a difficult situation. Because they have debt to refinance, they face the choice of selling shares to raise money or risking downgrades in their credit-ratings that will increase their interest payment burden.

---

[17] Cowell, Alan, "France Telecom Trims Sale of Orange Shares", *International Herald Tribune*, November 29, 2000, p. 17.

Already in 2000, credit rating agencies such as Moody's Investors Services Inc. downgraded the long-term ratings of several European phone companies. For example, it cut France Télécom's rating in September from Aa to A. The French phone giant had sold debt worth €5 billion in September, but now says it will generate some €25 billion from the Orange flotation and from asset sales over the next 18 months. If the sale of shares in Orange does not raise as much cash as planned, France Télécom will have to offset the shortfall through additional sales of other assets.

DIGGING ITSELF A DEEPER HOLE?

Despite its difficulties, France Télécom SA recently agreed to take control of Equant NV, a Dutch operator of a huge data communications network, in a deal worth almost $4 billion. Equant will be combined with France Télécom's Global One division to create a new force in corporate telecommunications services. France Télécom hopes to gain economies of scale in data networking, which could help it compete with giants like British Telecommunications PLC and AT&T Corp.

For Equant, which had a loss of $61 million in the first nine months, double its loss last year, joining France Télécom will bolster its existing network. Equant was started in 1995 by transforming an airline reservation system into a global communications provider. Besides offering voice, data and Web hosting services, in 2000 Equant joined Reuters PLC to establish a system called Radianz. Radianz provides a secure Internet network for financial services companies.

France Télécom has agreed to acquire the 34 percent of Equant owned by SITA, an airline consortium, for €3.5 billion ($2.9 billion). France Télécom then will merge its Global One assets with Equant and invest an added $1 billion in return for Equant shares, thereby increasing its stake to 54.3 percent of the combined company. The aim appears to be to create a new global services division within the company.[18]

In a complex, two-phase operation, France Télécom first will sell its corporate data business to Equant for cash and Equant shares, and acquire SITA's shares in Equant in exchange for France Télécom shares. The combined companies earned $3 billion in revenue in 2000, and expect annual savings of as much as $400 million before taxes by the third full year of operation.[19]

For France Télécom, it was the latest in a series of acquisitions intended to increase its presence in the highly competitive telecommunications market. By paying for Equant with shares, France Télécom avoided an increase in its own debt level. Next, France Télécom gained full ownership of Global One when it paid $4.3 billion to buy out Sprint and Deutsche Telekom, with whom it had created Global One in 1996. France Télécom's alliance with Deutsche Telekom fell apart in 1999.

---

[18] Tagliabue, John, "France Télécom to Acquire Equant", *International Herald Tribune*, November 21, 2000, p. 19.

[19] Ibid.

SITA, short for the Société Internationale de Télécommunications Aéronautiques, had been looking to get out of its initial investment in Equant for some time. Equant shares had dropped by about 70 percent during 2000, as the effort yielded no result. Subsequent to the deal's announcement, Equant shares soared by more than 20 percent, while France Télécom's stock price fell more than 4%, probably reflecting the growing burden on the latter's balance sheet.

GERMAN CONCERN IN DIFFICULTY

Another telecommunications giant, MobilCom also finds itself in difficulty. Its stock price has sagged from over €140 to under €70. That is a small catastrophe for those investors, who had purchased shares at their highest price of about €200 in the spring of 2000. The reason for the price decline is the prospect of huge losses, which firms like MobilCom will have in the near future. Together with its 28.5 percent minority partner, France Télécom, MobilCom paid almost DM16.5 billion for a UMTS-license. Due to the abovementioned further billions in investment for network construction, MobilCom therefore will be deeply in the red at least through 2006. Many experts regard even this scenario, though, as too optimistic.[20]

The dissension among analysts with regard to MobilCom's prospects illustrates their uncertainty about how lucrative this new business will be for network providers. Some of them predict a short-term price for MobilCom stock of just €50 per share, while other experts foresee a price of over €150. As always, when the market is uncertain, rumors abound. According to one rumor, the enterprise is so strapped for cash it plans to sell its Internet subsidiary, Freenet. Or: MobilCom's CEO wants to resign. Or: he already has sold his MobilCom shares to France Télécom. MobilCom regularly denies everything. However, it recently caused additional confusion with the announcement it would go to court over the UMTS-license fee, albeit without returning the license. No one outside MobilCom seems to understand this move.

Due to the controversy surrounding UMTS, many people have lost sight of the fact that the present-day telecommunications business itself is fraught with considerable risk. Indeed, with over 10 million customers in a growing market, MobilCom is one of the most successful German mobile telephone operators. But downwardly spiraling prices for services are depressing the industry's margins. In the first six months of 2000, MobilCom doubled its sales revenue to more than DM2 billion, but its profit of DM29 million was down over 60% relative to the same period in the prior year. In addition, image problems threaten MobilCom. The concern has made a name for itself not only through aggressive advertising, but also through bad service.

If analysts still view MobilCom shares at all positively for the long-run, that has to do with France Télécom's option until the year 2002 to buy a majority interest in MobilCom. If shares remain as cheap as they are at the moment, and the former can raise

---

[20] Mattauch, Christine "Eine Frage des Preises: Der Telefon-Aldi MobilCom gerät an der Börse unter Druck," *Die Zeit*, 12. Oktober 2000, p. 37.

the necessary cash, the option likely will be exercised. Thus, at least for MobilCom shareholders, there appears to be something of a safety net on the downside of its stock price.[21]

OTHER CONCERNS IN DIFFICULTY

Just over a year ago, British Telecomuunications PLC was under fire for, of all things, having too little debt. Analysts urged the former state-run monopoly to borrow money and make acquisitions to keep pace with its competitors. So it bought minority stakes in two mobile-phone operators, SmarTone Telecommunications Holdings Ltd. in Hong Kong and LG Telecom Co. in South Korea. It also invested in Cegetel SA, the French telecommunications group, and in Airtel Movil SA of Spain. In a sign of how drastically times have changed for telecommunications companies, BT now is considering selling many of those assets to reduce its debt, which otherwise will triple to £30 billion ($43.59 billion) by the end of 2001.

BT is not alone in its strategic aboutface. Royal KPN NV, Deutsche Telekom AG, France Télécom SA and almost every other significant player also are scaling back their amibitions in the face of soaring costs for third-generation mobile-phone licenses. Apparently, the previous strategy of being big is no longer viable. These companies therefore need to compromise their strategies, which should lead to substantial belt-tightening in the near-term.

Such backpedaling is one reason why European telecommunications stocks are unlikely to regain their former lofty levels any time soon. An index of these stocks has dropped 47 percent from its 12-month high in March, and analysts hold out the possibility that the $770 billion in market value eliminated in that slide could be gone for good. Before the European auctions for third-generation licenses – whose final cost totaled about €140 billion ($117.80 billion) – the ratio of capital expediture to sales for major telecommunications companies averaged 15 percent and was declining. Factoring in the long-term cost of these licenses and amortizing them over 10 years, the ratio jumps to 20 percent. That increase, which measures the rising cost of doing business, should translate into a permanent 35 percent reduction in the market value of these companies.[22]

Even as investors digest the increased costs of financing new services like mobile commerce, it remains unclear whether the concerns will be able to finance the strategies they have paid for so dearly. The amount of money telecommunications companies are trying to raise over the next few months is unparalleled. In the fourth quarter alone, Telecom Italia SpA, BT and France Télécom are trying to raise as much as $25 billion in debt, or three-quarters the amount issued by all European telecommunications companies through the first nine months of the year. Stock issues, meanwhile, are expected nearly to

---

[21] In contrast, Deutsche Telekom's merger with Voicestream will be voided, if the former's share price falls below €33.

[22] Kapner, Suzanne, "European Telecom Firms Backpedal," *International Herald Tribune*, November 1, 2000, p.16.

double in 2000, to $180 billion from $100 billion the previous year, with almost half the increase coming in the fourth quarter.[23]

After 18 months of throwing money at the sector, investors have begun to show signs that they have had enough. The spreads, or differentials, between telecommunications bonds and government securities are widening – not just for high-yield issues, but for investment-grade debt too – as investors demand higher returns for bearing the growing risks associated with financing costly new services.

Furthermore, huge equity deals like the sales of shares in Teléfonica Moviles SA of Spain and France Télécom's Orange unit have been delayed and likely will go forward only at reduced levels. Because a growing portion of these stock deals involve a parent company's selling shares in a subsidiary in which it retains control, some analysts and fund managers have become even more wary.

One case in point is that of Deutsche Telekom, which argued that selling shares in T-Online AG would allow it to offer managers of the Internet portal greater incentives through stock options tied closely to that subsidiary's performance. Instead, many T-Online executives left the company, saying they were stifled by Deutsche Telekom's control. Since going public in April 2000, T-Online shares have fallen 34 percent. Investors increasingly seem to be asking themselves why, if these subsidiaries are so good, does the parent company want to sell parts of them to the public?

Clearly, one reason is to pay down debt. Although these companies already have seen their credit ratings lowered, further downgrades are likely if they do not reduce their debt. Such lower ratings would increase borrowing costs and reduce financial flexibility still further. In this kind of situation, it then becomes more difficult to carry out acquisitions and mergers.

So companies that a short time ago thought nothing of buying their way into a market are becoming choosier. A few weeks ago, for instance, France Télécom abandoned merger talks with the Dutch data network operator Equant NV, citing unfavorable market conditions.

CONSEQUENCES FOR SOME OTHER EUROPEAN COUNTRIES

Belgium plans to auction off four next-generation mobile-telephone licenses this month. Learning from the British, Dutch, and German sales and their fallout, it has established both an entry fee and a series of qualifications for the bidders. The licenses each will last 20 years.[24]

Elsewhere, East European governments are trying to raise at least $5.5 billion from selling licenses for new high-speed wireless technology to companies already stretched by the cost of building initial mobile-phone networks. Poland, the Czech Republic and Hungary reportedly are eager to sell permits for systems enabling Internet access from

---

[23] Ibid.

[24] N.a., "Very Briefly:", *International Herald Tribune*, September, 7, 2000, p. 15.

handys. However, Eastern Europe's hurry to copy the West could backfire. The companies most likely to bid, many part-owned by foreign partners such as Deutsche Telekom AG, are completing costly, GMS wireless networks that already represent advanced technology for the former communist countries, or spending heavily on West European UMTS-licenses and networks.

Nevertheless, Poland already has set a starting price and specified how it would spend the resultant revenue. Some observers believe that the Poles have made too many compromises in rushing to begin their auction. Consequently, the planned auction well might collapse.[25]

But the region does not want to wait. The revenue the countries hope to raise from selling licenses for the next generation of technology rivals their biggest state asset sales since communism collapsed a decade ago. Poland aims to raise $3.8 billion in the bidding for its licenses, more than the government has received from any sale of state assets except the July sale of a stake in Telekomunikacja Polska SA, the national phone company, to France Télécom SA and a partner for more than $4 billion.

The Polish government already has earmarked the expected proceeds from its UMTS-auction for social spending – mainly to cover state employees' wages and health-care costs – for the next two years after setting a minimum price of €750 million ($644.6 million) each for five permits. Essentially the current mobile phone operators in Poland, as in other countries, have no choice but to participate in order to be certain they can introduce the new technology. Competition from foreign rivals will be limited because many are strapped for cash following the West European auctions, with sales in Italy and France still to come. Companies without a mobile network, such as Poland's Netia Holding SA, may not be able to find financing. Accordingly, Poland has made a gesture to potential bidders, agreeing to allow installment payments over several years.

The Czech government likewise aims to raise at least 20 billion koruny ($492.9 billion) selling four licenses in 2001, while analysts expect the sales could bring in as much as $1.4 billion. The government wants to use most of that revenue for education. If analysts' estimates are correct, proceeds from the sale of Czech UMTS-licenses could exceed receipts from the 1995 sale of a 27 percent stake in Cesky Telecom AS, the national phone company, to KPN NV and SwissCom AG for $1.45 billion. The government is counting on a successful UMTS-license auction after it was forced to delay the sale of a further 51 percent of the national phone company following KPN's decision not to increase its stake.

Following Germany's auction success, Hungary now is considering selling its UMTS-licenses in 2001 instead of 2002. It is likely that Hungary will sell four licenses for about $300 million each. The estimated revenue to be raised, about $1.2 billion, far exceeds Hungary's biggest state asset sale, the 1993 sale of a stake in Matav Rt., the national phone company, for $875 million.

The speedy auctions mean there will be no reprieve for such West European telecommunications concerns as Deutsche Telekom and France Télécom, whose

---

[25] Den Broeder, Adri, "License Sale Mania Hits Eastern Europe: Strategy Could Backfire Analysts Warn," *International Herald Tribune*, September 13, 2000, p.15.

spending power already has been diminished by West European license costs. To continue pursuit of its pan-European network strategy, Deutsche Telekom will have to back UMTS-license bids in 11 East European countries. Furthermore, it must do so even as it faces falling profit at home and spends more than $40 billion to buy Voice-Stream Wireless Corp. in the United States. All the same, the German company is doubling its stake in Polska Telefonia Cyfrowa SA, Eastern Europe's biggest wireless company, to 45 percent. It already controls Hungary's Matav and is increasing its stake to a majority of RadioMobil AS, the second-largest Czech mobile phone company. It also owns stakes in phone companies in Slovakia and Ukraine.

ITALY'S AUCTION FIASCO

The last major West European sale of 3G UMTS-licenses ended with a whimper when Italy's auction of five permits raised only €12.2 billion. That was just half of what the government and most analysts had expected. While the lower-than-expected results mean less money for the Italian government's coffers, they cheered Europe's mobile telecommunications industry. By marking the end of the auction phase, the Italian sale effectively set a ceiling on operators' license fees, enabling them finally to get on with the business of network construction.

But the promise of 3G still faces huge hurdles. Mobile phone firms, which will pay a total of more than €140 billion ($117.80 billion) for licenses in Europe, will have to spend as much again over the next five to seven years to build the networks. At the same time, the disappointing experience with today's mobile Internet services using the Wireless Application Protocol (WAP) has raised doubts about whether there ever will be sufficient consumer demand to make those investments profitable.

The Italian government, which had counted on proceeds of €25 billion to reduce the massive national debt a bit, called a quick ministerial meeting amid speculation it might annul the auction result. That prompted the chief executive of the Internet company Tiscale SpA, a member of one of the winning bidding consortia, to warn that any such move would be scandalous.

The result also raised serious questions about British Telecommunications PLC's business strategy. The auction ended when Blu SpA, a mobile operator in which BT and Autostrade SpA each hold a 20 percent stake, dropped out of the bidding. That followed the refusal of several other members of the Blu consortium to increase their bids. The move was a serious blow to BT's ambitions of developing a pan-European network to rival Vodafone and companies like Deutsche Telekom AG and France Télécom.

In addition, Italy's public prosecutor's office subsequently opened an inquiry into Blu's alleged manipulation of the government's auction process. Accusing Blu of collusion, it said it would fine the joint venture ItL4 trillion ($1.72 billion) by retaining its deposit and would seek further damages. Blu replied with a statement strongly rejecting the suspicion of incorrect behavior, failure to follow rules, or violation of the auction's reserve obligations.[26]

The license winners are Telecom Italia Mobile SpA, Italy's biggest mobile operator; Omnitel Pronto Italia SpA, which is backed by Vodafone Group PLC; Wind SpA, a joint venture of the state utility Enel SpA and France Télécom SA; IPSE 2000 SpA, which is backed by Telefónica SA of Spain and Andala SpA, backed by Hutchison Whampoa Ltd. of Hong Kong and Tiscali SpA. Shares of several of those companies rose sharply after Blu dropped out.

The Italian result underscored the wide variety of market conditions that have produced dramatically different auction results across Europe. In Italy, the high degree of market concentration held down prices. Together, Telecom Italia Mobile and Omnitel control nearly 90 percent of the handy market, making it difficult for competitors to gain a foothold. Furthermore, Italian mobile users spend less (a monthly average of €34) than their counterparts elsewhere in Western Europe (a monthly average of €40). That significantly decreases the opportunity for new entrants in Italy relative to other markets.[27]

The result leaves France as the last major market to select third-generation licensees. As previously explained, France will award its licenses in 2002 at a fixed price of €4.96 billion each. The fixed-price method had looked like an attempt to favor French bidders at a significant cost to taxpayers when the French government announced the process in May. But in light of results like Italy's, the French fees no longer look cheap.

SWITZERLAND'S AUCTION FIASCO

A second auction fiasco occurred in Switzerland's much smaller market in November 2000. There, officials abruptly postponed the sale of new-generation mobile telephone licenses after the number of bidding companies dwindled enough to jeopardize the government's expected receipts. The last-minute decision further darkened the clouds over the telecommunications industry in Europe.

Swiss regulators delayed the auction after Tele Danmark A/S said it had bought control of two bidders, Sunrise Communications SA and Diax Holding. The move left only four companies bidding on four licenses. Last August, 10 companies had been accepted to bid, but Teldotcom AG, Deutsche Telekom AG, Telenor Mobile Communications AS of Norway and Hong Kong's Hutchinson 3G Europe dropped out and only SwissCom AG, Orange Communications SA, Telefónica SA of Spain and Diax-Sunrise were left as the auction was set to begin.

Despite the country's small population, the Swiss government had anticipated a lucrative sale because of its affluent and telecom-savvy population, with high per-resident

---

[26]N.a., "Angry Italy Accuses Phone Firm of Cheating," *International Herald Tribune*, October 25, 2000, p. 13.

[27] Buerkle, Tom "Hammer Lands With Dull Thud In European Phone Auctions", *International Herald Tribune*, October 24, 2000, p. 1.

mobile phone and Internet use. The minimum bid for each Swiss license was set at $28.36 million. But Swiss authorities had hoped the auction, which was to be held over the Internet, might raise as much as $5 billion. A noncompetitive sale left officials facing the prospect of a much lower gain.[28]

Bakom, the Swiss telecommunications regulator, subsequently said it wanted to investigate the circumstances of the bidding companies' withdrawals to find out whether they were voluntary or if there were any indications that unlawful agreements had been made. The bidders expressed unhappiness with the Swiss decision, disputing Bakom's statement that the delay was merited by major changes in the structure and ownership among the bidders.

SwissCom said it would consider taking legal action if the authorities called a new auction for the 15-year licenses because that likely would lead to a higher price per license. Just in advance of the auction, Vodafone Group PLC had taken a 25 percent stake in SwissCom's mobile phone unit. SwissCom is the country's former phone monopoly. Bakom indicated that it probably would decide by year-end what course to pursue.

CONCLUSION

Can American firms exploit the disarray that has arisen among European telecommunications concerns to regain lost ground in 3G-mobile telephony? At present, the outlook is not encouraging because the U.S. government has delayed distribution of the requisite frequencies. The problem is the chaos reigning in America's airwaves, a result of generous public goods giveaways in the past. The frequencies the United States needs for its mobile telephone industry are thus extraordinarily scarce. Currently, they still are being used by television stations, whose rights don't expire until 2006. Former FCC-Director Reed Hundt recently warned that this problem could cost the country hundreds of billions of dollars.[29]

---

[28] Olson, Elizabeth, "Swiss Postpone License Auction," *International Herald Tribune*, November 14, 2000, p. 15.

[29] Lütge, Gunhild, "Hoch gepokert – und nun?", *Die Zeit*, 17. August 2000, pp. 17-18.

Chapter 3

THE EUROPEAN EMPLOYMENT PACT - AN ANALYSES OF THE INITIATIVES AND THE POSSIBILITIES OF A COORDINATED EMPLOYMENT POLICY

H.-D. Hardes
University of Trier, FRG

THE EUROPEAN EMPLOYMENT PACT (EEP)

According to common understanding, a pact is a contractual relationship, a binding promise of related persons, groups or states. Hence the wording (introduced during the German presidency) describes various developments of initiatives which have been ignited by the European Council at the summits in Cardiff, Luxembourg and Cologne. The aim of these initiatives is to foster employment and growth in the EU. They are supra-national processes of co-ordination between the member states of the EU, which are going to be developed further over time. The initiatives do not compel the member states to take certain measures, nor are they legally binding. Keeping this in mind, they are processes of an international economic coordination, enforced by the development of the European monetary and currency policy.

Under the EEP, three initiatives or parts can be distinguished:

♦ a macroeconomic dialogue to coordinate the general economic policy, i.e. stabilization policy, monetary policy, fiscal policy and the development of wages,
♦ a coordinated employment strategy with common supra-national guidelines to foster work and employment combined with national action programs and
♦ a number of proposals for structural reforms to catalyse economic growth in the EU

Fig.1: The elements of the EEP

European Employment Pact (EEA)		
Makroeconomic Dialogue	**Coordinated Employment Strategy**	**Structural Reforms**
Coordination of targets for the policy mix of macroeconomic growth and stability: *monetary policy, fiscal policy, dynamics of wages*	*common guidelines,* evaluation *National Action-Plans* (for promotion of employment)	deepening of the Internal Market: deregulation, reduction of subsidies support of small enterprises, infrastructure, information technology

From the combination of these three initiatives, aiming primarily at improving the global employment quota, one can conclude that the European Council targets intensifying and mutually re-enforcing effects in the various fields of economic policy support and an overall coordination of economic policy.

As such, the EEP is a heterogeneous program of an institutional coordination between numerous actors spread over different fields of policy from which complementary and mutually re-enforcing effects are expected.

METHODS FOR A COORDINATION

The coordinated employment strategy implies common strategic targets in the form of supra-national common guidelines for an employment policy to be able to influence national measures of an active employment policy. The processes for a coordination embrace the following core areas of an active promotion:

◆ the re-integration of jobless people (employability concept)
◆ the dynamics of the demand for work or entrepreneurship
◆ the flexibility and adaptability of employers and their employees
◆ equal opportunities and the integration of certain groups which face disadvantages on the labor market.

Within this framework, the member states are going to put more emphasis on actively promoting labour and employment as well as implementing measures to support such a promotion. As a first step, the European Council introduced certain agreements on the level of the EU and its member states (Luxembourg, November 1997), e.g. quantifiable targets (based on results within member states applying "best practices"), qualitative recommendations based on a qualified majority vote of the European Council, result-oriented, medium-term action programs in the member states (following the principle of subsidiarity) and regular multi-lateral review and evaluation processes.[1]

The European Council thus recognised the primary responsibility of the member states. Especially the national governments are given the responsibility via institutional processes. Where labor market organizations model and influence vocational training, education of employees and microeconomic conditions of employment, they are asked to participate in the process of coordination.

The macroeconomic dialogue for coordinating the general economic stabilization policy has various dimensions: the independent European Central Bank (ECB) is responsible for the supra-national monetary policy. The main aim of the ECB is to guarantee price stability. As long as the European economic policy does not threaten price stability, the ECB supports the economic policy of its member states (Art. 105 (1), EC-Treaty).

Fiscal policy is an area of common interest in the EU. Nevertheless, the respective national institutions are responsible here. In order to achieve a multi-lateral coordination of national fiscal budgets, the national secretaries of states (ECOFIN) must follow the guidelines of the Stability and Growth Pact. The nature of the Stability and Growth Pact differs to that of the EEP: it compels the member states more strongly to comply with its provisions. A continuous supervision of the fiscal budgets through ECOFIN will spot excessive national deficits and may initiate sanctions against respective member states. To judge what an excessive deficit is, quantifiable ex-ante provisions were introduced as a framework for a decision of the European Council. The provisions still allow for taking into account specific individual circumstances with regard to a member state. Even before any macroeconomic dialogue takes place, the fiscal policy must already comply to the provision of the Stability and Growth Pact and aim at a consolidated budget in the medium-term.

As a consequence, a macroeconomic dialogue must develop within the framework of certain existing national political guidelines, the ECB's supra-national, independent policy aiming at price stability and the *regular provisions*[2] of the Stability and Growth Pact. Wage policy is also part of this framework: taking into account the different wage bargaining systems in the member states, the right of free collective bargaining is never to be questioned. The general development of wages in the member states is mentioned as a relevant measure for the macroeconomic stabilization policy, not any particular system of bargaining.

---

[1] For further details about the targets (guidelines) and processes of a common employment policy see Hardes, 1999, pp. 209

[2] Procedures of regular coordination have to be differentiated from discretionary coordination. In the case of the latter the actors prefer decisions which are related to the actual situation and vary from case to case. The regular coordination includes ex ante-rules of the future behaviour of the actors.

Hence the coordination of the macroeconomic policy mix is more similar to an open process of a periodic dialogue (i.e. conferences) between numerous actors from the political and economic environment.

Open questions remain, especially with regard to a coordination of the monetary policy and other areas of the stabilization policy: what does the sub-ordinated responsibility to support the economic policy of the EU really mean?

The problematic role of the fiscal policy on the EU-level remains: the absence of a central fiscal policy may create a vacuum within areas of the growth and stabilisation policy on the EU-level. An enlargement of the EU towards the East calls for a system of a supra-national redistribution of financial revenues.

The integration of wage policy into the policy mix to support stabilization remains questionable altogether. It remains unclear which role a wage policy has within an employment policy and how macroeconomic wage strategies can be implemented effectively.

In the third part of the EEP, the structural reforms to foster growth, activities are concentrated on the planning and implementation of common, long-term programs. One example are projects which focus on the internal market, e.g. a reform of subsidies allowing for more competition, a reform of the infrastructure policy to promote transnational infrastructures, and common science and technology research programs. Specific project planning and project coordination is emphasised. Not every member state favors a common approach in structural and technology policy, not at least because of doubts of market order policy ("Ordnungspolitik") and absent provisions about who can overtake responsibilities during the implementation phase and who is paying for the structural reforms.

The overall aim of the EEP is an "all-embracing" institutional coordination within three political domains: a coordinated macroeconomic stabilization policy including monetary policy, fiscal policy and wage policy, the promotion of economic growth from a European perspective and measures of and active employment policy based on the supply side of the labor market. The ability to improve the level of employment in the EU thus depends on complementary relationships between the macro-policy, the economic growth and a coordinated policy for the promotion of employment. Within the framework of a monetary union, these political domains should be coordinated to catalyse positive employment dynamics throughout the EU. The necessary procedures to achieve such a coordination are of a supra-national, multi-lateral nature. Numerous actors from different areas have to participate.

There are various methods of coordination, e.g. some compulsory regulations with regard to the public deficit, and procedures to coordinate the targets of the national employment policies. However, compulsory elements in the policy mix are rare and the relevant actors have not made any concrete promises. The central monetary policy within the European Monetary Union (EMU) is the core element of mostly open procedures and multi-lateral efforts to coordinate actions in the various policy areas.

THE REASONS FOR STRATEGIC EFFORTS
TO COORDINATE POLICY ACTIONS

Basically there are two arguments for a general supra-national coordination:

-   especially because of general interdependent effects between the policy areas (the employment policy, the macro policy and economic growth) with mutually complementary relationships;
-   furthermore specific spillover effects of national initiatives within a fiscal policy or employment policy between the member states of a monetary union exist.

The *fiscal policy argument* belongs to the second category, i.e. that supra-national financial transfers in a monetary (and political) union are unavoidable. Within a community of various nations with a common fiscal policy, the concrete forms of horizontal and vertical financial transfers are debatable, but the general necessity of transfers in a political union is widely recognized.

In a monetary union with a common monetary policy for the whole currency area asymmetrical shocks and unequal economic developments in the regions are very likely. One can assume, that the absence of a national differentiation of the monetary policy on the one hand and the absence of a central budget and a supra-national redistribution of financial revenues in the EU on the other hand will make it much more difficult to compensate for national or regional unequal economic developments.[3] As a consequence different regional cyclical and growth effects will occur. Intra-industrial trade relations within the EU or the extra-EU trade may reduce some regional differences, but different economic developments in the member countries cannot be completely excluded. One cannot expect a convergence of national budgetary policies.

There are two reasons for spillover effects within fiscal policy:

-   national budgets will affect common interests,
-   international financial transfers are necessary in the case of economic crises.

The Maastricht treaty stresses the national responsibilities for the fiscal policy area, because the economically weaker members states should not regard the monetary union as an "implicit insurance against illiquidity".[4] A supra-national liability for excessive debts of national states or regional administrative bodies is excluded in Art. 104b of the Maastricht treaty. The regulations of the Stability Pact should furthermore induce budgetary discipline.

---

[3] "If wages are rigid and if labour mobility is limited, countries that form a monetary union will find it harder to adjust to demand shifts than countries that have maintained their own national moneys ... It also helps to form a monetary union if the budgetary process is sufficiently centralized so that transfers can be organized smoothly (...) between the countries of the union" (Grauwe, de, 1997, S. 11).

[4] Hagen, von, 1993, S.287

Nevertheless the "no bail out"-clause will not prevent increasing supra-national transfers in the EU. If the member states want to preserve their goal of a political union, higher international transfers are much more likely. Therefore the "no bail out"-clause appears to be incredible, if EMU is considered as a prologue to a political union.[5] A process of differentiation in fiscal policy between the members states will cause increasing international transfers in the case of an economic crisis, i. e. it will lead to spillover effects or externalities within a monetary union.

Similar arguments can be used concerning a *wage policy*. In a monetary union with a common currency national prices and wages are directly comparable. Employees in particular nations can compare their wages with those in other EMU-countries: a monetary illusion caused by different national currencies no longer exists. The requests for *equal wage for equal work* will widen and be more emphasized in both the public discussions and wage bargaining.[6] If these requests can be realized, wages will expand much stronger in the peripheral, economically weaker countries of the EU. The pressure on labor costs to increase will grow stronger over-proportionally at given labor productivity rates. Such an expanding development of national labor costs in the weaker member states will then deepen the problems of unemployment. The concequence will be a regional clustering of unemployment.[7]

Similarly to the effects in the fiscal policy such an scenario in the wage policy would lead to international spillover effects heading for a union of financial transfers. In such a case the calls for supra-national transfers would grow wider, as the regional clusters of unemployment in the economically weaker member states would ask for the introduction of structural funds, i. e. a stronger support following the principle of solidarity between the member states.

Apart from these effects of the requests for equal wages, there are major institutional differences in the wage policies among the member states: the structures of bargaining and the forms of institutional organisations differ. Following the general understanding such institutional differences influence an adaptation also in the case of symmetric shocks. After national policy instruments of a monetary and currency policy have become obsolete, the costs of adaptation for alternative instruments in the monetary union increase.[8] As a consequence the pressure for an institutional reform of the wage policy will grow in all participating states.. The latter belongs to another category of arguments for a coordination of employment policies: complementary effects in various areas of a policy mix.

---

[5] The Maastricht treaty excludes a bail out de jure, but it will be difficult, to create a common understanding for the compulsory nature of this clause. A monetary union could be regarded as a pre-stage of a political union, which will also ignite a corresponding solidarity in the fiscal policy between the members (Beck, 1997, p. 97).

[6] Compare the request for equal wages during the German monetary integration.

[7] Unemployment will increase where wage levels are higher than productivity levels and where differences in the levels of productivity are not taken into account by the bargaining parties. This applies especially to the economically weaker countries, i. e. those economies whose productivities are relatively low compared to the average level, especially in Portugal, Spain and the new *German Länder* (SVR, 1998, no. 3,6).

[8] Grauwe, de, 1997, pp. 25.

In the area of macro policy there is the question of a coordinated policy mix between the monetary policy on the one hand and the national fiscal and wage policies on the other. According to the Maastricht treaty the primary goal of the ECB is to secure monetary stability. The treaty also provides for the political independence of the ECB, except in the area of currency policy in relation to non-member states. Opinions differ whether the treaty also requires the ECB to support employment policy. At least the Postkeynesions propose an active role of the ECB. They deny the classically based hypotheses that only unexpected inflation can cause short-term effects on employment and that hence a central bank has an "inflationary bias"[9] with a primary short-term perspective. Accordingly, a central bank can mainly influence interests by controlling short-term market interests rates. Thus it indirectly influences interest rates at the capital markets and of investments. With a time lag inflationary effects and effects on demand are caused through these transmission channels. At the same time such an interest policy influences the long-term expectations for the development of inflation rates by the actors of the market. From the perspective of the Postkeynesians monetary policy is primarily a reaction to short- and long-term market developments, and can only be effective if the actors in the fiscal and wage policy collaborate. As such a central bank would normally be more likely to apply a restrictive instead of an inflationary monetary policy.[10] Influencing and controlling the effects of monetary policy in connection with the markets and together with the actors from other policy areas is therefore a major problem in the tasks of a central bank. Slight changes of interests may cause only weak reactions of the markets, while major changes may cause economic recessions later on. On the other hand a policy of low interests rates may cause cyclical effects of employment if wage and fiscal policy do not act against these effects. A coordinated macro policy which aims for consensus among the relevant actors will be more effective than singular measures. The complementary nature of such a process of coordination is a major reason for a coordinated macro policy.[11]

Finally this text deals with the connection between a coordinated employment strategy and a macro policy. The EEP asks for a coordination between active measures to promote employment and a macroeconomic dialogue. This seems reasonable if the various components of cyclical unemployment - influenced by macroeconomic variables - and structural unemployment cannot be exactly distinguished. The first major goals of the coordinated strategy of employment policy in the EU mainly aim at a better re-integration of long-term unemployed through individual consulting and training initiatives for example. The EEP targets more intensive measures to promote employment following best practice examples in particular Scandinavian countries in combination

---

[9] For the microeconomic foundation of the above mentioned inflationary bias of the actors in monetary policy see Barro/Gordon, 1986, pp. 589-610.

[10] "Central bankers have typically ... a positive bias against monetary expansion and (will, suppl.) implement monetary politics tied to much longer-run considerations, even if these are politically costly ... in the short run" (Spahn, 1999, p. 385; see also p. 394).

[11] For the role of economic and political complementary effects in employment policy see Orszag/Snower, 1998, pp. 303.

with a macro policy that also supports employment targets. The latter should be negotiated by a process of macroeconomic dialogue. The macro policy should reduce the cyclical component of unemployment. The coordinated employment strategy should reduce the structural component of long-term unemployment according to the "employability"-concept. Insofar the EEP apparently assumes a complementary relation between the cyclical and the structural component of unemployment or mutually effective relations of the two components.

A corresponding diagnosis implies that one cannot distinguish correctly between the causes for cyclical and structural unemployment. Important explanations could be based on hysteresis - and selection processes during a cyclical increase of unemployment.

Hysteresis effects, i. e. if unemployed people lose their human capital and their motivation to look for work, will evolve in the case of long-term unemployment. Long-term unemployed can thus become outsiders with a low "employability".[12] The fact that long-term unemployed are more likely to be insufficiently qualified can also be explained by selection processes during the fluctuation of the unemployed. In the case of decreasing demand for labor a gap between the average qualification of outsiders and those of insiders will emerge.[13] In other words: during high and increasing unemployment it will be more and more difficult to re-integrate the long-term unemployed.

Therefore there are a number of reasons to support a general multi-lateral effort to coordinate national employment policies under the EEP, especially from a New-Keynesian perspective. The chances of a successful institutional implementation of an international co-ordination remain debatable, however.

CHANCES AND PROBLEMS OF A PROGRAM OF MULTI-LATERAL COORDINATION

This paper has characterized the EEP as a general but heterogeneous, international effort to coordinate various areas of policy, with different procedures of a coordination and different prerequisites. Can such a multi-lateral program of an institutional coordination with numerous and heterogeneous participants be successful, especially as the various roles and responsibilities of the relevant policy actors remain unclear? The doubts mainly concern the open procedures of the macroeconomic dialogue and the coordination of the strategic targets of the national employment policies. Especially a functional integration of the wage policy and the bargaining institutions appears vague at the moment. After the experiences of the Social Dialogue based on the Protocol of Social Policy in the appendix of the Maastricht treaty and Art. 139 of the Amsterdam treaty, a major short-term success is very unlikely. The wage policy throughout EMU will make it even more difficult for the EEP to succeed as it will increase the pressure for a microeconomic decentralization instead of a European coordination.

---

[12] See f. e. Blanchard/Katz,1997, pp. 68; Hardes, 1999, p. 207.

[13] Spahn, 1999, pp. 397

The academic discussion does not deny the necessity of a microeconomic decentralization of the wage policy, even if there are differences concerning the functional consequences with regard to the promotion of more employment of such a process of decentralization. Apart from the globalisation processes the monetary union will increase the necessity of these processes of decentralization between external provisions (outside the companies) and internal flexibility. Already at the beginning of the Sixties *Mundell*, in his theory of optimum currency areas[14], had pointed out that asymmetric shocks or different reactions in the participating countries of a monetary union asked for adaptation processes in the following areas:

- relative prices between domestic and foreign countries,
- the wage structures, or
- the mobility of labor.

The latter is not sufficiently existent in Europe to fulfill such a function of adaption. Therefore in a monetary union the inter-regional and inter-company functions of the allocation of wages will increase, i. e. a decentralization of the bargaining policy will have to occur.

As well, the discussion about the connections between the degree of centralization of wage bargaining and the macroeconomic performance leads to similar conclusion based on the Calmfors-Driffill hypothesis:[15] The European integration by the Single Market and the monetary union strenghtens the demand for a decentralized bargaining policy. However, opinions differ about the concrete forms of such a decentralized wage bargaining policy, its range and functions. The new classical paradigm exclusively regards the reduction of unemployment as a problem of a microeconomic tuning of the labor markets via differentiated and flexible wage structures in the member states. In their opinion the macroeconomic implications for the assignment of the various roles in employment policy are obvious. Especially they will hold the bargaining partners responsible for reducing cyclical and structural unemployment in Europe. This would imply that the decentralization of the wage policy as a strategic element of employment policy would solve problems of unemployment: a competitive coordination of the wage policy via a decentralization to the company level is necessary. Any further forms of an institutional coordination would be unnecessary.[16] On the contrary the New-Keynesian school promotes a supplementary macroeconomic coordination of the wage policies, besides the decentralization, e. g. as in the form of the macroeconomic dialogue proposed by the EEP. The only instruments for a coordination between the development of wages, the monetary and the fiscal policy are a regular dialogue (conferences) between the

---

[14] Mundell, 1981, p.657

[15] For the hump-shape hypothesis and the consequences of the European integration for the bargaining policy see Calmfors, 1993, pp. 161.

[16] We do not support a common European bargaining policy. Such a tendeney would prevent a differentiation of wages within the monetary union and counteract a necessary flexibility in the wage structures (SVR, 1998, no. 322). See also Berthold/Hank, 1999.

European social partners without "compromizing on the autonomy of the bargaining partners and on the diversity of national bargaining systems"[17]. The wording of the EEP allows for a non-compulsory process of multi-lateral exchanges between the relevant institutional representatives. It does not contain provisions concerning possible procedures and results of an institutional coordination. The initiators of the EEP obviously recognized that the implementation would be difficult. On the European level there are no functional structures of corporatism, as they exist in smaller counties of the EU, e. g. in Scandinavia or the Netherlands. Such corporatist structures are unlikely to develop because of the institutional diversity of national bargaining organizations and the structural features of the wage bargaining processes. Furthermore the bargaining partners are bounded by the different interests of majorities among their members. These institutional features counteract an internal conversion of guidelines into concrete demands and results in decentralized bargaining processes. Furthermore it seems unrealistic to expect that a macroeconomic dialogue will result in centralized bargaining procedures on a European Level. This applies equally to fears from the Neo-classical side.

Firstly, a process of a European dialogue to coordinate national employment policies would have to concentrate on defining the functions of the dialogue within the new framework of a monetary union. A common bargaining policy has hardly been mentioned so far. As a start the general implications of the monetary union and common, more specific targets of an employment policy should be negotiated throughout a dialogue. Some examples of relevant problems and questions have been mentioned above:

-   Within the macroeconomic dialogue the partners could negotiate a common point of view concerning the possible demand of "equal wages for equal work" in a monetary union.
-   It is generally accepted, that globalization and the monetary union require forms of decentralization in national bargaining policies. A macroeconomic dialogue could point out possible options of such a decentralization, based on respective country reports.
-   The centralization of monetary policy has shifted the weight towards the supra-national level in this area. As spillover-effects result from this dominant role of the monetary policy for other areas, the principal relations between those areas should become a subject of the dialogue.

These options should only serve as examples. They point out that a target-oriented dialogue to answer questions of a basic significance still has to be developed. The functions of various forms of coordination within a commonly guided employment strategy and a macroeconomic dialogue need to be part of the agenda. The absence of clear institutional procedures and responsibilities throughout an international coordination may cause mis-management or more unnecessary and routinized conference activities.

---

[17] See European Commission, 1999, pp.2.

LITERATURE

Barro, Robert J./Gordon, David B. (1982):»A Positive Theory of Monetary Policy in a Natural Rate Model«, in: *Journal of Political Economy*, Vol. 91 (1983), pp. 589-610

Beck, Reiner (1997): »*Stabilitätspolitik in der Europäischen Wirtschafts- und Währungsunion. Der geld- und fiskalpolitische Policy-Mix im Europa von Maastricht*«, Baden-Baden

Berthold, Norbert/Hank, Rainer (1999): »Bündnis für Arbeit: Korporatismus statt Wettbewerb«, *Bd. 159 der Beiträge zur Ordnungstheorie und Ordnungspolitik*, ed. by the Walter-Eucken-Institut, Tübingen

Blanchard, Olivier/Katz, Lawrence, F. (1997): »What Do We Know and Do Not Know About the Natural Rate of Unemployment«, in: *Journal of Economic Perspectives*, Vol. 11, pp. 51-72

Calmfors, Lars (1993): »Centralisation of Wage Bargaining and Macroeconomic Performance«, in: *OECD Economic Studies*, No 21, pp. 161-191

European Commission (1999): »Bericht an den Europäischen Rat (Köln) über die Ausarbeitung eines Europäischen Beschäftigungspakts«, *Pressemitteilungen*, No. 8705/99, Brüssel;

Grauwe, Paul, de (1997): »*The Economics of Monetary Integration*«, 3. ed., Oxford

Hagen, Jürgen, von (1993): »Monetary Union and Fiscal Union: a Perspective from Fiscal Federalism«, in: Masson, Paul R./Taylor, Mark, P. (ed.): »*Policy Issues in the Operations of Currently Unions*«, Cambridge, pp. 264-296

Hardes, H.-Dieter (1999): »Zur Frage der Notwendigkeit einer strategischen Koordinierung der Beschäftigungspolitik in Europa«, in: *Mitteilungen aus der Arbeitsmarkt- und Berufsforschung*, 32. Jg., pp. 203-218

Mundell, Robert A. (1981): »A Theory of Optimal Currency Areas«, in: *The American Economic Review*, Vol. 51, pp. 657-664

Orszag, Mike/Snower, Dennis J. (1998), »Anatomy of Policy Complementarities«, in: *Swedish Economic Policy Review*, Vol. 5, pp. 303-343

Sachverständigenrat zur Begutachtung der gesamtwirtschaftlichen Entwicklung (SVR) (1997): »Jahresgutachten 1997/98«, *Bundestagsdrucksache* 13/9090, Bonn

SVR (1998): »Jahresgutachten 1998/99«, *Bundestagsdrucksache* 14/73, Bonn

Spahn, Heinz-P. (1999): »Central Bankers, Games and Markets. A Critical Assessment of the Microeconomic Optimization Approach in the Theory of Macroeconomic Stabilization«, in: Filc, Wolfgang/Köhler, Claus (ed.): »*Macroeconomic Causes of Unemployment: Diagnosis and Policy Recommendations*«, Bd. 36 der Veröffentlichungen des Instituts für Empirische Wirtschaftsforschung, Berlin, pp. 379-403.

Chapter 4

THE EU SOCIAL POLICY DILEMMA: COMPETING ECONOMIC AND SOCIAL OBJECTIVES

Nick Adnett
Staffordshire University Business School, UK
Stephen Hardy
Manchester School of Management, UMIST, UK

ABSTRACT

The agreement to modernise EU Social Policy at the Lisbon Summit represents a further stage in the reappraisal of the European Social Model begun in the Treaty of Amsterdam. In that Treaty economic and social objectives were more directly juxtaposed. EU policymakers in the post-Amsterdam era have faced a major dilemma: which objective should have precedence, economic or social? In this chapter, we investigate this dilemma, analyzing EU's policies on employment security and labour market flexibility. We concentrate on two particularly relevant case studies: the 1977/1998 Acquired Rights and the 1993 Working Time Directives. We consider whether the legal confusion associated with these Directives can be attributed to any conflict between EU policy goals or the differing models of implementation and enforcement adopted by individual EU Member States Governments. In drawing conclusions, we directly address the implications of our analysis for the modernization of EU Social Policy.

INTRODUCTION

A continuing objective of European economic integration has been to promote both economic and social cohesion, an objective now formalized in Article 2 of the Treaty of the European Union. At the March 2000 Lisbon Summit the need to modernize EU Social Policy was agreed, though the Portuguese Presidency preferred the term 'renewal'. In this modernization process, policymakers once again face a central dilemma – on what basis to trade-off economic and social objectives when they are mutually incompatible.

This chapter considers the present legal confusion associated with this dilemma and its implications for the reform of EU Social Policy. The examination concentrates particularly upon the impact of the Acquired Rights Directives (ARD) which govern business transfers, and the Working Time Directive (WTD) which enforces restrictions on working hours. The significance of the ARD for our analysis is that it explicitly recognizes that economic, technical or organizational considerations may justify the withholding of social rights. In the case of the WTD, the significance lies in its widespread use of derogations and the encouragement given to the social partners to negotiate exemptions. We wish to analyze whether separately or together these Directives provide any lessons for the redesign of EU Social Policy.

The consolidated version of the Treaty of Rome 1957 (as amended 1992, 1998) affirms that the essential objective of the Community is to constantly improve living and working conditions whilst recognising the need to remove barriers to balanced trade and fair competition. The Treaty of Amsterdam introduced a new Employment Chapter into the E.C. Treaty: the objective of maintaining a high level of employment is now required to be taken into consideration when Community policies and activities are formulated (Article 127). More specifically, social policy directives are to be designed so as to avoid hindering the creation and development of small and medium-sized undertakings (Article 137). At the 1997 Luxembourg 'Jobs' Summit a common employment strategy was agreed with specific targets being transposed into policies in each Member State in annual National Action Plans for Employment. The March 2000 Lisbon Summit decided that EU Social Policy needed to be modernized along lines compatible with the employment guidelines of the Luxembourg process. How the continued commitment to strengthening the social rights of EU employees is to be reconciled with the increased entrepreneurial freedom implied by this championing of more flexible labour markets is the problem now facing EU policymakers.

In the following section we outline the historical origins of the present policy dilemma and assess orthodox analyses of the need for EU Social Policy reform. The third section examines the nature of business transfers in the EU and provides a review of relevant case law. This review explains how the European Court of Justice (ECJ) has failed to provide consistent rulings on the applicability and implications of the Acquired Rights Directives, especially for the extension of market-based reforms in the public sector. The penultimate section addresses the Working Time Directive in a similar fashion. Here we examine whether derogations and the encouragement of negotiated opt-outs provide a solution to the problem of how to prioritize economic and social objectives. The final section discusses the implications of our findings for the redesign of EU Social Policy.

THE EU SOCIAL POLICY DILEMMA: HISTORY AND ANALYSIS

The economic history of the European social model has recently been re-interpreted by Eichengreen and Iversen (1999) reflecting the current anglo-centric orthodoxy. Strong European economic growth after the Second World War was based upon Fordist technology supported by solidaristic wage bargaining. Whilst centralized wage bargaining compressed the distribution of wages and was associated with the growth of welfare programs and labor market regulation, the effects of these policies were sustainable given the prevailing production technologies. With the emergence of flexible specialization and the growth of holistic firms, the prevailing labor market institutions and employment regulations no longer sustained the EU's competitiveness in the fast growing sectors of the global market (Gual, 1998). The perceived over-expansion of welfare and regulation was now identified as a cause of chronic unemployment amongst the unskilled, falling male participation rates (through early retirement and permanent disability), and slow employment growth in the high-tech and service sectors (OECD, 1994).

The establishment of EMU has intensified the concern that an EU Social Policy based upon leveling-up may be inconsistent with increased economic integration and continuing international competitiveness (Bean et al, 1998). As Otmar Issing (2000), a member of the Executive Board of the European Central Bank, recently argued what orthodox economics indicates is required instead is greater labor costs variability between, and within, EU labor markets. Though perversely, integration itself tends to promote both greater wage interdependence and wage convergence (Andersen et al., 2000). Finally, globalization has been identified as a further reason why Social Europe is no longer sustainable. The growth of trade and capital mobility increases labor cost elasticity of demand for labor and rigidities in wage adjustments increase the employment consequences of regulating labor market behaviour. In extending this argument, Saint-Paul (1997) argues that Europe's rigid labor markets encourages a concentration on producing a small range of relatively secure goods and services at a late stage of their product life cycle. A specialization associated with low market growth, low innovation, low learning externalities and therefore generating a low potential for European economic growth. As international trade and capital mobility increase, an international product cycle becomes established with specialization in new goods and services in those economies with decentralized wages and 'employment at will'.

In the UK the consensus that 'old-style' social democratic economic policies had failed to produce their desired objectives of full employment and a more egalitarian distribution of income and wealth led to a long period of neoliberalist-inspired reforms under Prime Minister Thatcher. Since 1997 a Labour Government has attempted to develop employment and welfare policies based upon a 'Third Way' (Giddens, 2000). From this perspective traditional social democracy had elevated rights above responsibilities, whilst 'modernizing' social democrats now recognized that the modern globalized, knowledge economy required a different steer. The resulting advocacy of regulation for competitiveness has enabled both some convergence of national policies within the EU and the Lisbon agreement to modernize the European Social Model (Adnett, 2000).

Even prior to the creation of the EC the neoliberalist or employment-at-will approach had been effectively rejected by Continental European economies for the conservative-corporatist model. A rejection based predominantly upon political and social, rather than economic, grounds. In a world of perfectly competitive labor markets, legal and institutional restrictions are either completely ineffective or prevent the signing of socially efficient contracts between workers and firms. In such markets only equity considerations provide a rationale for regulation. In practice, the presence of both monopoly and monopsony power (Gregg and Manning, 1997), incomplete contracts and asymmetric information (Cartier, 1994 and Parkin, 1996) and hence the importance of trust and co-operation (Wilkinson, 1998) all provide potential complementarity between economic, or more accurately efficiency, considerations and social protection. Within this framework employee rights assist in creating high average tenure in the labor market which encourages socially advantageous investments in human and physical capital by employers and employees (Deakin and Wilkinson, 1994). This belated economic rationale for the European Social Model was partially adopted in the analysis contained in the EU Commission's 1993 White Paper, 'Growth, Competitiveness, Employment'.

As we have noted, persisting mass unemployment in the EU and the perceived employment successes of the US-style flexible labor markets have led to a critical assessment of the European Social Model. However, Freeman (1996) summarising the findings of a major cross-country study of labor market regulations, noted that the flexible labor markets of North America whilst performing well in terms of employment growth performed poorly, when compared with more regulated labor markets, in terms of productivity growth and wage inequality. New technology has generated new economies of scale and scope, which together with the effects of increased competition in product markets has encouraged firms to adopt new employee management systems such as 'lean production' and Total Quality Management. Marsden (1996, 1997) and Brown and Rea (1995) point out that these systems increase the importance of co-operative industrial relations and the need for rules and rule-making procedures to manage collective discontents. The European Social Model provides regulations and institutions which encourage long-run trust relations as well as providing a forum for adapting behaviour to this new environment. It follows that in order to encourage employees to co-operate in adjusting employment practices to fast changing market conditions some restraints on entrepreneurial freedom, such as requiring the transfer of acquired rights, may be needed. More (1995) argues that other flexible employment practices, such as contracting-out, are often motivated by a desire to gain competitive advantage from avoiding employment regulations themselves, rather than to exploit new technological or market opportunities. Together these arguments suggest that a modernized EU Social Policy can be designed in which economic and social rights become complementary in an economic system devoted to sustaining and creating high productivity employment. The following analysis of the Acquired Rights and Working Time Directives investigates the problems that arise in seeking to achieve that complementarity in practice.

THE ACQUIRED RIGHTS DIRECTIVE

The 1998 Acquired Rights Directive, amending the original 1977 Directive, embraces the need to both clarify the scope and purpose of the law regulating business transfers. As a minor success of the UK's Presidency of the Council of Ministers, the Amending Directive inserts new Articles 1-7b into the original Directive clarifying its scope, information/consultation requirements and its applicability in the case of insolvency. However, the term 'business transfer', or *'transfer of undertaking'* as it is legally known, remains the same and means at its simplest level, a change of ownership of 'any trade or business', either commercial or otherwise. This general definition adopted by the original ARD, excludes share transfers, due to the overwhelming political pressure amongst the EU Member States at the time of its drafting. The ARD was in part motivated by the fear that national differences in labor law would distort competition in the common market. As Hepple (1997) explained, it was expected that increased trade would directly increase pressure on both companies based within and outside Europe to restructure and that this process would be concentrated in countries where existing workers had no right to the continuation of their previous terms of employment. The EU's Single Market initiatives provided an additional stimulus to business transfers and a further factor has been the trend for governments to privatize and contract-out services previously produced within the public sector.

Since 1985, the ECJ has given nearly forty rulings on the ARD and by 1990 the ECJ had become embroiled in clarifying whether the ARD did apply to certain business transfers or not, mainly attempting to exclude those business transfers which occurred under a regime of contracting-out. This is evidenced by the important ruling from the ECJ, that of *Schmidt* (1995). Following its previous rulings in *Rask* (1993) and *Spijkers* (1986), the ECJ in *Schmidt* ruled that the contracting out of a single cleaner came within the scope of the ARD. In particular, the absence of tangible assets and the fact that it is an ancillary activity and performed by a single employee were not deemed decisive factors for the purpose of establishing a business transfer. The significance of the German case of *Schmidt* was the ECJ's conclusion that the retention of the job's original identity post-transfer 'is the decisive criterion for establishing whether a transfer' has occurred.

Comparisons of these rulings of the ECJ suggested a central question of: whether the cessation of a specific operation within an undertaking and the consequent transfer of that operation to an outside undertaking, is to be regarded as a transfer of a part of the undertaking within the meaning of the Directive? A question which was answered in the affirmative, when the ECJ held contracting-out to be clearly within the scope of the ARD. In *Rask*, a case concerning the tendering of the operational running of a canteen service, the ECJ had affirmed the 'retention of identity' test and categorically included CCT within the scope of the Directive. The ECJ's 'robust' jurisprudence surrounding the ARD seemed at this stage to be clarifying the muddied legal waters caused by contracting-out across the EU.

The *Schmidt* judgement was met with strong criticism from many EU governments. In particular, some German lawyers refused to accept that an activity could be transferred without a transfer of goodwill and business knowledge. The impact of such case law upon German labor law has been analysed by Korner (1996), who suggests that German scepticism on EU labor law regulation is rooted in a belief that "EU-provisions challenge the very structure of German labor law " (p. 3). Such reasoning might reveal not only why so much of the ECJ's litigation on the ARD has been of German origin, but also explains the political nature of the controversy surrounding the ARD.

Tracing the catalogue of caselaw, Hardy and Adnett (1999a) argue that the *Suzen* case brings the legal turmoil to a head. In that case, a contract to clean a church-run secondary school in Bonn was terminated with one contractor and awarded to another, giving rise to eight dismissals on the grounds of redundancy. The ECJ argued that the mere fact that the service provided by the old and new contractor is similar, did not mean that a business transfer had taken place. The ECJ held in *Suzen* that a transfer of activities was insufficient to amount to a transfer of an undertaking, reaffirming the orthodox 'economic entity' test which had been developed in *Spijkers* and later refined in *Schmidt*. Thus, no relationship need exist between the transferor and transferee prior to the transfer for the ARD to apply, but the passing of tangible assets or the taking over of a workforce remain as pre-requisites for meeting the *Spijkers* test. Had the ECJ followed the Advocate-General's advice, the *Suzen* decision would have impacted on all contracted labor-only services. Since a vast majority of public sector cases in the EU today involve such, as does most other contracting-out, then this ruling should not trouble many EU labor lawyers, contractors, unions and employees.

More recently, as observed by Hardy & Painter (1999), a softening of the Suzen decision is given by the ECJ in *Hernandez Vidal v. Gomez Perez & Others*. Here the approach lays emphasis on what the undertaking looked like pre-transfer and as a result reduces the possibility that a transferee can evade the social regulation. The ECJ held that "an organised grouping of wage earners who are specifically and permanently assigned to a common task may, in the absence of other factors of production, amount to an economic entity".

Our survey of the existing case law records how the EU political debate surrounding the battle between social and economic rights has entered the legal ambit. The introduction of the stable economic entity test suggests that the economic roots of business transfers can water-down the extent of the social protection afforded by the ARD. Consequently, the EU's legal processes have allowed the ECJ to effectively modify the ARD in line with changing economic situations over the last two decades. As a result, Community law as an instrument of social policy consents to the upholding of worker's employment protection rights, whilst curtailing those rights in line with the current trend towards 'market flexibility' by way of preserving 'entrepreneurial freedom'. Although, this was not the case in *Deutsche Telekom AG v. Vick* where the ECJ used upheld worker's rights in pursuit of social policy goals by stating: *"The social aim of article 119 of the EC Treaty (now article 141 EC) must prevail over its economic aim so the article did not preclude legislation enacted by a member state which risked adversely affecting the competitive situation of economic operators in that state"*. This case involved an equal pay claim and illustrates that evidently the ECJ can decide between social and economic rights. The dilemma raised by the ARD could have been anticipated given that this Directive explicitly recognises the potential conflict between economic and social rights in its specification of its economic, technical and organisational defences for employers. Article 4 of the ARD provides that a: *"...transfer of an undertaking, business or part of a business shall not in itself constitute grounds for dismissal by the transferor or the transferee. Furthermore, this provision shall not stand in the way of dismissals that may take place for economic, technical or organisational reasons entailing changes in the workforce"*. This provision makes the dismissals of employees by either the purchaser or the vendor automatically unfair unless the reason for these dismissals are for 'economic', 'technical' or 'organisational' (ETO).

Although there are, as yet, no direct EU precedents on the ARD's ETO defences, two other rulings of the ECJ shed some light on the EU's likely interpretation of these defences. Firstly, Advocate-General Darmon in *Bork* (1989) suggested that the ETO defences were restricted where *"...the undertaking's resumption of business was envisaged"*. This declaration has led the ECJ to believe that the applicability of the ETO defences is narrow, and most certainly inapplicable should the business continue post-transfer. Following this advice, the ECJ held that Article 4(1) of the ARD shall not in itself constitute grounds for dismissal and that the employees transferred were to be treated as still employed, albeit now by the transferee.

Similarly, the ECJ's reluctance to rule on these ETO defences directly is seen in respect of insolvency proceedings. For example, in *Abels* (1985) it was stated that whilst accepting that the ETO defences apply to liquidation scenarios, that even:*"...if a viable part of a business in liquidation is sold off, there may be no valid economic grounds for dismissing any of the staff employed in that part of the business"*. In its ruling in *Bork*, the ECJ in considering whether there had been a dismissal where the ETO defences applied, declared that *"...account had to be taken of the objective circumstances in which the dismissal occurred..."*. The ECJ's view appears to be that the ETO defences are not automatically granted and in the circumstances in which they apply should be adjudged objectively in the facts of the instant case. This legal position was recently reaffirmed by the ECJ in the case of *Jules Dethier Equipement SA* (1998), where the Court held that:*"Article 4(1) of the Directive gives the transferor, as well as the transferee, the power to dismiss employees for economic, technical or organisational reasons. Inasmuch as Article 4(1) precludes dismissals from taking place solely by reason of the transfer, it does not restrict the power of the transferor any more than that of the transferee to effect dismissals for the reasons which it allows"*.

From the British experience, as observed by Hardy & Adnett (1999a), it is now clear that the ETO defences can apply to dismissals and redundancy situations, but whether these defences are applicable clearly depends upon how these terms are interpreted. Though whilst the ARD fails to define them, the British Government in 1993 issued guidance. The UK Government defined 'economic' to mean "where a demand for an employer's output has fallen that profitability could not be sustained" (Waldegrave 1993 paras. 14-15); 'technical' referred to the usage of "new technology and the employees did not have the necessary skills"; and described 'organisational' as a situation which arises "where a new employer operates at a different location and it is not practical to relocate".

At present, Community law provides insufficient guidance on these important defences. Consequently, after twenty years of case law on the ARD the conflict between economic and social rights following business transfers remains unresolved by the courts across the EU and within the ECJ itself.

THE WORKING TIME DIRECTIVE

The EU's Social Affairs Council adopted the Working Time Directive (WTD, Directive 94/104/EC)) in 1993 under Article 118a (now Article 138) of the Treaty on the European Union. The main provisions of this Directive were aimed at limiting maximum hours of work, and establishing minimum entitlements to rest periods and paid annual leave for most workers in the EU. This initial resistance to this new social measure was based upon orthodox economic theory, which argues that competition forces employers to agree working hours in line with the preferences of individual employees (Addison et al., 1997). Employers who find it expensive to match these preferences will, in order to recruit and retain workers, have to provide compensation in the form of higher wages. Thus the theory of compensating wage differentials predicts that most individuals will be working their utility maximising number of hours conditional on their wage. Imposing working time restrictions must therefore lower workers' utility and raise employers' unit labor costs, thereby reducing the competitiveness of EU producers.

The debate concerning the proposed WTD was typical of many within the Community at that time. The then British Government employed a liberal-individualist rationale to object to labor law standards that were based largely upon the Roman-Germanic European norm. However, over the decade since that debate both European labor markets and the global economic environment agendas have changed and we noted above how as a consequence economic and social policy-making are more directly juxtaposed. The growth of intra-EU and global competition has increased pressure on employers to increase working time flexibility and make existing working time structures cheaper (for example, by eliminating overtime and unsociable hours payments). Whilst, European trade unions have historically pursued an opposing strategy: bargaining for reductions in straight-time weekly hours and, effectively, increased overtime hours. In recent years, some groups of workers have voluntarily conceded the more flexible working arrangements demanded by employers. Customized working time arrangements often better matching their educational, family and lifestyle commitments. New forms of work organization, such as annualized hours and work on call, are making working time more heterogeneous and individualized. As such the sort of social rights as defined in the WTD appear dated and the need now is to distinguish more clearly between work and free time (Supiot, 1999).

As Adnett and Hardy (2000) argue despite having minimum standards set out on hours, rest, night work and holidays, a number of derogations, including a total derogation from the Directive, provide flexibility and freedom of contract for employers and employees. For instance, derogations initially came in the form of exemption from the Directive for trainee doctors, passenger transport employees and sea-going vessels workers and range into areas of working time regulation, such as recording and consent to work beyond the nationally set limit. In some respects, therefore, the WTD anticipated the type of more flexible EU Social Policy championed in the Treaty of Amsterdam and again at the Lisbon Summit. From a different perspective these derogations and negotiated exemptions potentially enable circumventive evasion amongst employers with strong bargaining power.

The Directive provides a legal framework in an area of employment law where, as Fajertag's (1998) survey shows, most EU Member States already had national working hour legislation which were more restrictive than the WTD. It may therefore be thought that the Directive would cause little confusion or litigation. However, the first problematical area within this Directive is its central definition of 'working time'. Working time being defined as *"any period during which the worker is working at the employer's disposal and carrying out his activity or duties in accordance with national laws or practice"*. Herein lies the problem: transposition. In particular, national regulations can allow for employees and employers to make a 'relevant agreement' to clarify what constitutes working time and rest periods. Agreements could also be collectively agreed or specific to certain workers, as opposed to the whole workforce (Bercusson, 1996). There is nothing in the Directive that covers second or additional employment. A further anomaly in this EU legislation is that both rest periods and night work are related to 'shift work'. The latter is defined in the Directive as *"any method of organising work in shifts whereby workers succeed each other at the same workstation according to a certain pattern which may be continuous or discontinuous"*. Such terminology appears to provide a great deal of flexibility. Though, the Directive imposes an obligation on employers in planning work organisation to *"take account of the general principle of adapting work to the worker with a view in particular, to alleviating monotonous work and work at a predetermined work-rate depending on the type of activity and of health and safety requirements especially as regards breaks during working time"* (Article 13). No derogation of this article is possible. As Bercusson (1994 and 1996) observed such an obligation requires employers to consult their workers, and/or their representatives, where they intend to change work patterns in order to ensure a 'humanising' approach to work, avoiding or minimising risks to workers' health & safety.

The desirability of negotiated derogations from the WTD can be questioned. If more flexible labor markets create greater employment insecurity, then workers' ability to resist employers' attempts to extend working hours, paid or unpaid, is reduced. Workers may be forced to agree to extend their current working hours to provide insurance against unstable work futures. Working in excess of their long-term desired hours allows employees to accumulate income reserves in anticipation of future spells of unemployment (Bluestone and Rose, 1998). Such increases in the volatility of an individual's working hours are unlikely to be privately or socially efficient. The decentralisation of both pay and working-time determination has also contributed to this tendency (Arrowsmith and Sisson, 1999). Stewart and Swaffield (1997) provide empirical support for this broad proposition. They report that over a third of British men work longer hours than they would wish at the prevailing wage, with the mean of desired hours for manual men being 4.3 hours per week less than the actual hours worked.

Similar concerns about reliance upon derogation originate from the perceived undesirable growth of unpaid-overtime working. This appears to be an increasingly common feature of managerial and professional work (Bell and Hart, 1998), with working long hours seeming to have a strong effect upon promotion prospects (Booth and Francesconi, 1997). Landers et al. (1996) argue that these tendencies may reflect inefficient 'rat-race' equilibrium. These are characterized by a tendency for promotion to be on the basis of commitment, ambition and propensity to work hard, which given asymmetric information may all be proxied by actual working hours. In such circumstances, adverse selection issues may encourage workers who desire short hours to adopt the camouflage of working longer hours at the current wage. Working hour norms may therefore become inefficiently long and fail to adjust to the changing demographics of the workforce. This selection process may have the effect of discriminating against those groups bearing a disproportionate amount of non-market activities, particularly mothers. Hence, the call for more 'family-friendly' employment practices in Europe and the recognition that extending derogations may be inconsistent with these objectives.

CONCLUSIONS

Contrary to the predictions of simple factor price equalization models and the fears of high social protection EU Member States, continued European economic integration appears to have produced no 'race to the bottom' (Andersen et al., 2000). Product market integration has itself, as yet, not created major macroeconomic pressures on wages, regulations or the welfare state. In general, international evidence suggests that if the EU wishes to maintain labor market institutions and social rights that have a net negative spillover effects on labor productivity then, depending upon the particular measure, the costs are absorbed in four ways. The adjustment is through falling nominal wages, rising consumer prices rise, depreciating exchange rates and/or depending upon the rigidity of the labor market, employment levels. The ability to sustain these costs over time depends crucially upon how the particular regulatory measure affects the dynamics of productivity growth and whether social solidarity is sufficient to ensure the acceptability of the resulting income redistribution. In the absence of empirical evidence on these factors we draw three main conclusions from our case studies as to the setting of guidelines for the reform process.

Firstly, in our discussion of both directives we noted how the lack of a binding precedent in the ECJ increases the importance of precise drafting. Whether or not specific social rights can be reconciled with the perceived needs of economic efficiency, it is clear that imprecisely drafted directives seeking to establish modern sophisticated social rights create confusion and uncertainty. This uncertainty distorts decision-making and reallocates resources away from welfare-enhancing production into welfare-redistributing litigation. The process which permits individual EU Member States to transpose directives into their national statutes places a further burden on the ECJ, contributing to additional legal uncertainties based upon unresolved conflicts between national and ECJ rulings. It should be noted that our neglect of the political context within which social policy decisions are taken has caused us to ignore possible reasons for, and benefits of, imprecise drafting. Where EU Member States cannot reach agreement, imprecise drafting may by-pass such difficulties in the short-run. Similarly, the power given to the ECJ to interpret directives may, in practice, represent a means of allowing flexibility in applying EC legislation in particular and differing circumstances. Overall, however, we believe that our case studies shows that the long-run efficiency costs of such equivocation are significant.

Secondly, if the EU is to reassess the existing social rights, and any proposed enhancements, more critically in terms of their impact upon economic efficiency, then it is important that appropriate measures of efficiency are specified. Allowing the courts to equate economic efficiency considerations with the short-term interests of individual employers is unlikely to sustain either a Social Europe, nor enhance Europe's long-run international competitiveness.

Thirdly, examination of both the ARD and WTD indicate that it may be premature to devolve the trading-off of social and economic rights to the social partners. Changes in the economic environment have weakened employee bargaining power and increased the pressures on trade unions to negotiate deals that favour insiders to the detriment of the unemployed, entrants and re-entrants. An increase in negotiated derogations from EU Social Policy is likely to increase the incidence of both 'rat-race' equilibria and economic and social exclusion.

While the ECJ seeks to moderate between economic and social rights on a case-by-case basis, the French Presidency of the EU have recently sought agreement for a newly revised Social Charter. Whilst this proposal amounts in practice to little more than a consolidation of existing social rights, the ensuing negotiations between Member Sates is providing an indication of the continuing diversity of opinion as to how economic and social objectives should be juxtaposed in a modernized Social Policy.

REFERENCES

Abels v. Administration Board (1985) ECR 469 ECJ.

Addison, J., Barrett, C. and Siebert W. (1997) The Economics of Labour Market Regulation, in Addison, J. and Siebert, W. (eds.) *Labour Markets in Europe: Issues of Harmonization and Regulation* (London: Dryden Press).

Adnett, N. (2000) Labour Market Reform and Employment Policy in the EU: Third Ways of Modernising the European Social Model, *Staffordshire University Business School Division of Economics Working Paper*, Number: 2000:06.

Adnett, N. and Hardy, S. (2000) Reviewing the Working Time Directive: Rationale, Implementation and Case Law, *Staffordshire University Business School Division of Economics Working Paper*, Number: 2000:08.

Andersen, T., Haldrup, N. and Sørensen, J. (2000) Labour Market Implications of EU Product Market Integration, *Economic Policy* April 2000, 105-33.

Arrowsmith, J. and Sisson, K. (1999) Pay and Working Time: Towards Organisation-based Systems? *British Journal of Industrial Relations* 37(1): 51-75.

Bean, C., Bentolila, S., Bertola, G. and Dolado, J. (1998) *Social Europe: One for All?* (London: Centre for Economic Policy Research).

Bell, D. and Hart, R. (1998) Working Time in Great Britain, 1975-1994: evidence from the New Earnings Survey panel data, *Journal of the Royal Statistical Society, A* 161(3): 327-48.

Bercusson, B. (1994) *Working Time in Britain: Towards a European Model* (London: Institute of Employment Rights)

Bercusson, B. (1996) *European Labour Law*, Butterworths.

Bluestone, B. and Rose, S. (1998) The Macroeconomics of Work Time, *Review of Social Economy* LVI (4): 425-41.

Booth, A. and Francesconi, M. (1997) *Career Mobility in Britain*, ESRC Research Centre on Micro-social Change, Mimeo.

Bork v. Foreningen (1989) IRLR 41 ECJ.

Brown, W. and Rea, D. (1995) The Changing Nature of the Employment Contract, *Scottish Journal of Political Economy,* 42(3): 363-77.

Cartier, K. (1994) The Transaction Costs and Benefits of the Incomplete Contract of Employment *Cambridge Journal of Economics* 18: 181-96.

Deakin, S. and Wilkinson, F. (1994) Rights vs Efficiency? The Economic Case for Transnational Labour Standards, *Industrial Law Journal*, 23(4): 289-310.

Deutsche Telekom AG v. Vick (2000), C-234-235/96, Unreported, 10 February 2000, ECJ.

Eichengreen, B. and Iversen, T. (1999) Institutions and Economic Performance: Evidence from the labour market, *Oxford Review of Economic Policy*, 15(4): 121-38.

Fajertag, G. (1998) Working Time in Europe: Current trends, in Wheelock, J. and Vail, J. (eds.) *Work and Idleness: The Political Economy of Full Employment* (Dordrecht: Kluwer Academic Publishers).

Freeman, R. (1996) Does it Fit? Drawing Lessons From Differing Labour Practices, in Gual, J. (ed) *The Social Challenge of Job Creation: combating unemployment in Europe*, Edward Elgar, Cheltenham.

Giddens, A (2000) *The Third Way and its Critics*, (Cambridge: Polity Press).

Gregg, P. and Manning, A. (1997), Labour Market Regulation and Unemployment, in Snower, D. and de la Dehesa, G. (eds.) *Unemployment Policy: government options for the labour market*, (Cambridge: Cambridge University Press).

Gual, J. (1998) The employment debate: employment performance and institutional change, in Gual, J. (ed.) *Job Creation: The Role of Labor Market Institutions*, (Cheltenham, Edward Elgar).

Hardy, S. and Adnett, N. (1999a) 'Entrepreneurial Freedom versus Employee Rights': The Acquired Rights Directive and EU Social Policy Post-Amsterdam, *Journal of European Social Policy* 9(2): 127-37.

Hardy, S. and Adnett, N. (1999b) Flexible Labour Markets and Employment Rights in the EU: Competitive Tendering, Business Transfers and the Revised Acquired Rights Directive, in Meeusen, W. (ed.) *Economic Policy in the European Union: Current Perspectives*, (Cheltenham: Edward Elgar).

Hardy, S. and Painter, R. (1999) 'Business Transfers, employers' strategies and the impact of recent case law', *Journal of Employee Relations* 21(4): 378-388.

Hepple, B. (1997), 'New Approaches to International Labour Regulation', *Industrial Law Journal*, p. 353.

Hernandnez Vidal SA v. Gomez Perez [199] IRLR 132 ECJ.

Issing, O. (2000) Europe: common money – political union? *Economic Affairs*, March 2000: 33-39.

Jules Dethier Equipement SA v. Dassy (1998) IRLR 266 ECJ.

Korner, M. (1996) 'The Impact of Community Law on German Labour Law : The Example of Transfer of Undertakings', European University Institute (EUI), Florence, Italy, EUI Working Paper LAW No. 96/8.

Landers, R., Rebitzer, J., and Taylor, L. (1996) Rat Race Redux: Adverse Selection in the Determination of Work Hours in Law Firms, *American Economic Review* 86(3): 329-48.

Marsden, D. (1996) Employment Policy Implications of New Management Systems, *Labour*, 10(1): 17-61.

Marsden, D. (1997) The 'Social Dimension' as a Basis for the Single Market, in Addison, J. and Siebert, W. (eds), *Labour Markets in Europe: issues of harmonization and regulation* Dryden Press, London.

More, G. (1995) The Acquired Rights Directive: Frustrating or Facilitating Labour Market Flexibility, in Shaw, J. and More, G. (eds) *New Legal Dynamicsof European Union,* Oxford University Press, Oxford.

OECD (1998) *Employment Outlook*, Paris: OECD.

Parkin, R. (1996) Optimal Employment Security: The Benefits of Labor Market "imperfections", *Journal of post-Keynesian Economics* 19(1): 61-72.

Pitt, G., & Fairhurst, J. (1998) Blackstone's Guide to Working Time, Blackstones Press;

Rask v. ISS Kantineservice [1993] IRLR 133 ECJ.

Saint-Paul, G. (1997) Is labour rigidity harming Europe's competitiveness? The effect of job protection on the pattern of trade and welfare, *European Economic Review* 41: 499-506.

Schmidt v. Spar-und Leikhasse [1995] ICR 237 ECJ.

Sindicato de Medicos de Asistencia Publica (Simpa) v. Conselleria de Sanidad y Consumo de la Generalidad Valenciana, C-303/98, ECJ.

Spijkers v. Benedik [1986] ECR 1119 ECJ.

Stewart, M. and Swaffield, J. (1997) Constraints on the Desired Hours of Work of British Men, *Economic Journal*, 107(March): 520-35.

Supiot, A. (1999) The Transformation of Work and the Future of Labour Law in Europe: A multidisciplinary perspective, *International Labour Review*, 138(1): 31-46.

Suzen [1997] IRLR 255 ECJ.

Waldegrave, W., Rt. Hon. (1993) Guidance to Market Testing, OPSS, Department of the
    Chancellor of the Duchy of Lancaster, London, HMSO.
Wilkinson, F. (1998) Co-operation, the Organisation of Work and Competitiveness,
    ESRC Centre for Business Research, University of Cambridge, Working Paper No.
    85.

Chapter 5

LOCATION ADVANTAGES AND INTER-REGIONAL PREFERENCES IN THE EUROPEAN UNION

D. Giannias
University of Crete, Department of Economics, Greece
P. Liargovas[*]
University of Patras, Department of Economics, Greece

ABSTRACT

This paper challenges the Neo-classical argument of regional convergence and builds upon the argument that location advantages associated with site-specific characteristics in each region create external economies and therefore consumer income differentials can persist over time. A theory is presented to model the effects of location and income differentials on interregional differences. Based on this theory we can determine whether location and income differences primarily reflect consumers' or firms' dominated responses. We apply this theory in order to determine the relative importance of location advantage and income differences as sources of regional disparities across the EU member states.

INTRODUCTION

Economists, geographers and policy makers have shown a great concern for the persistence of large disparities among different regions or countries in terms of economic and social performance. Neo-classical analysis supports that regional inequalities are due to consumer income differentials. With identical regions, perfect competition, full employment, constant returns to scale and perfect mobility of factors of production, output (and income) of different regions should tend to converge over time towards a steady state (Solow 1956).

[*] *Address correspondence*: Dr. Panagiotis Liargovas, 29 Patroclou St, Vrilisia 152 35, Athens-Greece, e-mail: pliargov@cc.uoa.gr

This view, was challenged by a number of growth models (Romer 1986; Uzawa 1965; Conslik 1969). These growth models concentrate on various forms of market failure which constitute a radical departure form the strong assumptions of neo-classical models. Imperfect mobility of labour, for example, can have perverse effects in terms of regional disparities to the extend that migration to fast-developing areas is usually led by the most dynamic and highly skilled members of the labour force in the lagging regions.(Myrdal 1957; Robson 1987; Prud'homme 1993). Furthermore, the existence of economies of scale and learning economies arising from the accumulation of human capital might lead to divergence in regional outputs per head (Van der Ploeg and Tang 1992).

In addition, the regional economics literature points to external economies such as location advantages associated with easy access to large markets, centres of administration and finance, and sources of skilled labour and technological knowledge (Krugman (1991); Krugman and Venables 1990). In this paper we build upon this argument by supporting the view that consumer income differentials can persist because some factors are inherently immobile, e.g., the environmental and climatic characteristics that are unique to a region. It is possible that several regions share the same site-specific characteristics, but it is unlikely that their distribution will be exactly the same.

Economic agents put their own value on a region, based on its location advantage. A firm, for example may find that its location in a region with easy access to large markets, centres of administration and finance, and sources of skilled labour and technological knowledge and a good transportation and telecommunication system saves time and reduces its production costs. This implies that this particular firm can offer relatively higher incomes to its employees and still remain competitive with other manufacturing companies located in lower-income regions since the location advantage of the region are offering it a cost advantage. Since office space and other facilities in the area are limited, the companies attracted by the location advantage of the region will increase the demand for both labor and office space. These increases in the prices of labor and office space will continue until in equilibrium they have completely offset the cost advantage of the region. Incomes and rents will vary across regions according to the value companies place on the location-specific attributes in each region and their ability to substitute between factors of production.

Consumers, on the other hand, consider the overall location advantage when they make decisions concerning the place they will live in. These characteristics refer to all aspects of the natural (e.g. parks, recreation, climate, air-quality) and non-natural (e.g. cultural, transport, public services, access to large markets, centres of administration and finance) environment of the consumer. The region, for example, with easy access to large markets, centres of administration and finance, and sources of skilled labour and technological knowledge and a good transportation and telecommunication system that offered a cost advantage to some firms may be attractive to consumers because of reduced travel time to work and/or reduced cost of shopping . Consequently, as more consumers move into the area, the supply of labor increases as well as the demand for housing. Thus rents increase and wages fall until individuals in equilibrium are no longer willing to accept moving to a region with a location advantage as a compensation for lower wages and higher rents.

The final income differentials between a geographical area with a location advantage and one without depends upon the relative size of the demand and supply responses to site characteristics. If incomes are observed to be higher in the area with a location advantage than in the other, then the firm's response dominates the rent determination process. If incomes are relatively lower in the area with a location advantage, then the consumer's response dominates the process. In both cases rents will be higher because both households and firms value a good transport system. Rents would be lower than in otherwise comparable geographical areas if the regional transport system was not important to both parties. Consequently, by observing relative consumer incomes and rents, or by observing other variables having a monotonic relationship with them, it is possible to identify whether a region's bundle of environmental and location advantage has a greater net effect on company location decisions or consumer location decisions.

We can then use this framework to identify EU member states according to the extend they are dominated by supply and demand responses to their net bundle of country-specific attributes. The countries are then classified into four groups based on the relative values of a country's per capita income and location advantage. These groups include firm dominated rich countries (high consumer income, high location advantage), firm dominated poor countries (low consumer income, low location advantage), consumer dominated rich countries (low income, high location advantage) and consumer dominated poor countries (high income, low location advantage). This identification is useful because it provides information about the relative attractiveness to consumers and companies of the total bundle of location and other attributes indigenous to each country. It also assists policy makers to formulate the best suited regional and urban policies in the EU.

Section 2 of the paper presents a theoretical model of the effects of location and income differentials on interregional differences. Section 3 uses this model in order to determine the relative importance of location advantage and income differences as sources of regional disparities across countries in the EU. Finally, section 4 offers some conclusions.

THEORETICAL MODEL

In modeling the relationship between the effects of location and income differentials on interregional differences it is assumed that consumers have identical tastes and skills and are completely mobile, migration is costless, capital is completely mobile, production technologies are identical across companies and exhibit constant returns to scale, and, finally, companies and consumers have chosen locations such that they could not be made better off by relocating.

In our analysis, regions or countries are fully described by a bundle of location and other attributes. These specify the location advantage index of a country or region, LA, which includes all aspects of natural and non-natural environment of a consumer's life. LA affects the utility of consumers, U(.), and the cost of production for firms, C(.). Individuals in these regions are assumed to consume and produce the numeraire good, X, which is a composite good with a price that is equal to one. Each consumer supplies one unit of labor and receives his income, I, in return. His income is assumed to be a function of the location advantage of the region, I = I(LA), and is spent on housing and the numeraire good. The rental price of a house is a function of the vector of housing characteristics, h, and the location advantage of the region, LA, that is, the rental price of a house is specified by the following function: P = P(h,LA). It is assumed that P(h,LA) = R(LA) h', where h' is the transpose of h, and R(LA) is the vector of implicit prices for each housing characteristic. An equilibrium must be characterized by equal utility for identical consumers and equal unit costs for firms across all regions.

A utility maximizing consumer solves the following optimization problem:

max U(h,X,LA)

with respect to h,X,LA

subject to I(LA) = R(LA) h' + X

where I(.) and P(.) are the equilibrium income and rental hedonic equations, respectively.

Let LA^*, h^*, and X^* be the solutions to the above utility maximization problem specifying, respectively, the region he will be, LA^*, the kind of house he will live in, h^*, and how much of the numeraire good he will be able to consume, X^*. As a result of it, we have that the income of the consumer will be: $I^* = I(LA^*)$, and the rent he will pay for his house is: $P^* = P(h^*,LA^*) = R^* h^{*'}$, where $R^* = R(LA^*)$. Equivalently, the problem can be stated in terms of an indirect utility function V(.) where,

$V(I^*,LA^*,R^*) = \max U(h,X,LA^*)$

with respect to h,X

subject to $I^* = R^* h' + X$

Equilibrium for consumers requires that utility is the same at all regions, that is, V(I,LA,R) = v, where v is a constant. This equilibrium condition implies that individuals in regions with better location advantage pay for it through reductions in real income in the form of higher rent and lower wage income.

A cost minimizing firm solves the following problem:

min I(LA) L + r K + R(LA) h'

with respect to L, K, h, LA

subject to X = f(K,L,h,LA)

where K is capital, L is labor, I(.), and P(.) are the equilibrium income and rental hedonic equations, respectively, r is the unit price of capital, and f(.) is a constant returns to scale production in K and L.

Let LA^*, h^*, K^* and L^* be the solutions to the above cost minimization problem specifying, respectively, the region the production activity takes place, LA^*, the kind of building or office the company will use, h^*, and how much of capital and labor will employee (K^*,L^*). As a result of it we have that the income that the company will pay to the consumer will be: $I^* = I(LA^*)$, and the rent he will pay for the building facilities it uses: $P^* = P(h^*,LA^*) = R^* h^{*'}$, where $R^* = R(LA^*)$. Equivalently, the problem can be stated in terms of a unit cost function C(.) where,

$$C(I^*,LA^*,R^*) = min\ I^* L + r K + R^* h'$$

with respect to L, K, h

subject to $X = f(K,L,h,LA^*)$

Equilibrium for producers requires that unit cost is the same at all countries, that is, C(I,LA,R) = c. If the overall location advantage of a region provides a net productivity advantage to firms, they will pay for it in terms of higher incomes and rents. Wages and rents in each region are finally determined by the interaction of the location decisions of households and firms.

The model described above is illustrated in Figure 1. The downward sloping curve in Figure 1, labeled V(I,LA;R), shows combinations of I and LA for which utility is equal to v. The slope of these curves is the trade-off that households are willing to make between wage income and location advantage for any given level of implicit prices for housing characteristics (R) and the given utility level v. Along each curve, the implicit prices of housing characteristics is fixed and the curves shift up (down) as the implicit prices of the housing characteristics increase (decrease). The implicit prices of housing characteristics in the region labeled 2 is greater than the ones in the region labeled 1, since individuals enjoying a higher location advantage at every level of income must have in equilibrium their utility equal to v, so that there is no incentive for moving to other regions.

Figure 1

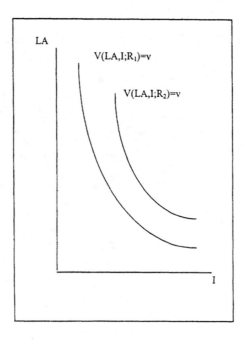

Combinations of LA and I for which the unit costs of firms are equal are depicted in Figure 2. The value of the location advantage of the region to firms is fixed along each iso-cost curve, and the curves shift up (down) as the location advantage of a region increase (decrease) the productivity of firms and the implicit prices, R, of the real estate market. According to Figure 2, the implicit prices in region 2 are greater than those of region 1, since firms facing a higher level of location advantage and having as a result a higher productivity at every level of wage income must have in equilibrium their unit cost equal to c, so that there is no incentive for moving to other regions.

Each region is characterized by a location advantage index and a vector of implicit rental prices that are associated with a specific pair of isocost and iso-utility curves as in Figures 1 and 2. The intersection of any two curves for each region at the level of its location advantage then determines the relative income and the implicit prices of the real estate market in equilibrium. In Figure 3, in region 1, where location advantage equals LA_1, the equilibrium income will be I_1 and the equilibrium implicit rental prices R_1. Using region 1 as a reference point, which could be thought as the average region, we can see in the following how interregional differences in location advantage will be reflected in differences in incomes and implicit rental prices.

Figure 2

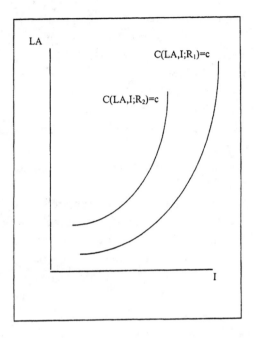

Figure 3

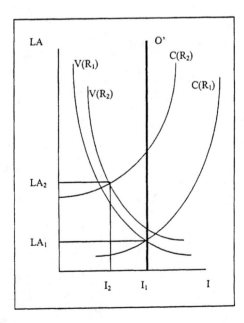

Consider a region 2 that differs from 1 only in that the location advantage of region 2 are valued more by consumers than the location advantage of region 1. This implies that, ceteris paribus, rents in region 2 will be relatively higher than rents in region 1. In Figure 3, this is illustrated by $V(R_2)$ lying above $V(R_1)$. Assuming there is no difference in location advantage between the two regions from the firms' point of view, we can see that equilibrium requires that incomes in region 2 be lower relative to region 1 and that $C(R_2)$ lies above $C(R_1)$ as shown in Figure 3. The higher rents and lower incomes reflect the amount consumers are willing to pay to locate in region 2 rather than 1 and, therefore, the location value of LA_2 relative to the average region. Moreover, since from the firm's point of view there is no difference in location advantage between the two regions, the effects of higher rents and lower incomes on costs offset each other so that unit costs remain in equilibrium equal to c.

Consider another region, region 3, that differs from 1 only in that the location advantage LA_3 provide a greater productivity advantage to firms. This implies that, ceteris paribus, rents in region 3 will be relatively higher than rents in region 1. This relationship is illustrated in Figure 4, where region 3 is represented by $C(R_3)$ which is to the left of $C(R_1)$. If no location differences exist from a consumer's point of view, we can see that equilibrium requires that incomes in region 3 are higher relative to region 1 and that $V(R_3)$ lies above $V(R_1)$ as shown in Figure 4. The higher rents and incomes reflect the amount firms are willing to pay to locate in region 3 rather than 1, and, therefore, the productivity value of LA_3 relative to the average region. Moreover, since from the consumer's point of view there is no difference in location advantage between regions 1 and 3, the effects of higher rents and incomes on the maximum utility of a consumer offset each other so that the maximum utility that a consumer enjoys in equilibrium remains equal to v.

Figure 4

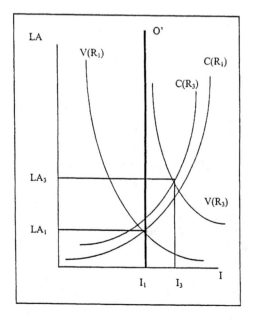

Putting the above cases of Figures 3 and 4 on the same graph, (Figure 5), it is seen that: (i) when location advantage is valued more by consumers, ceteris paribus, $C(R_2)$ and $V(R_2)$ have both been moved up and $C(R_2)$ has moved up relatively more, and (ii) when location advantage is valued more by firms, ceteris paribus, $C(R_3)$ and $V(R_3)$ have both moved up and $V(R_3)$ has moved up relatively more.

Figure 5

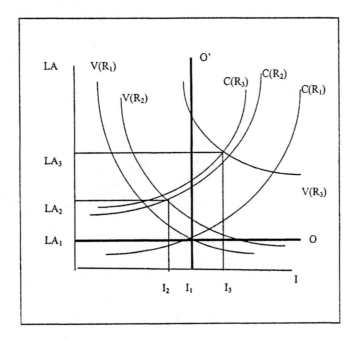

Within this framework in which regions differ only in their location advantage, we can determine whether location and income differences primarily reflect consumers' or firms' dominated responses. In the first case we would see a negative relationship between location advantage and incomes. In the second case, the relationship would be positive.

Within the same framework, we can also classify individual regions or countries on the basis of whether their incomes and location advantage differ from the average. These classifications are summarized in Table 1 and Figure 6. Location advantage is higher than the average in the firm dominated and consumer dominated rich countries and lower than the average in the firm dominated and consumer dominated poor countries. On the other hand, incomes are relatively higher in the firm dominated rich countries as well as in the consumer dominated poor countries.

Table 1

CLASSIFICATION OF REGIONS	DIRECTIONS OF DIFFERENTIALS		
	I	LA	SHIFT
Consumer Dominated Rich	Low	High	both curves up and C(Ri) relatively more
Consumer Dominated Poor	High	Low	both curves down and C(Ri) relatively more
Firm Dominated Rich	High	High	both curves up and V(Ri) relatively more
Firm Dominated Poor	Low	Low	both curves down and V(Ri) relatively more

Figure 6

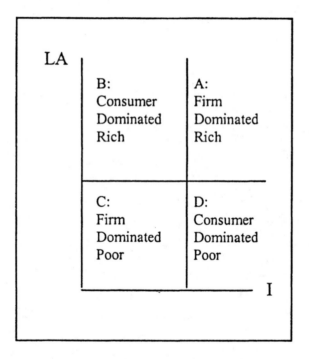

Each region is characterized by a location advantage index, LA, whose effect on household utility and production costs differs from region to region. The problem of classifying regions by the relative magnitude of these two effects becomes one of identifying the location and income differences in equilibrium relative to the shifts in each curve. This can be done by identifying the combinations of LA and I in equilibrium that are associated with equal shifts of both curves and determining how incomes and location advantage change relative to these shifts. The (LA,I) equilibrium combinations associated with equal shifts of both curves would coincide with the LA_1O and I_1O' lines in Figure 5, 6, and 7, where LA_1 is the mean location quality and I_1 is the mean income.

Figure 7

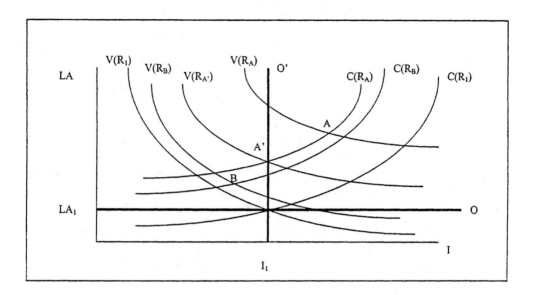

For any region with above average incomes and location advantage, the shift of the C(R) curve must be less than the shift of the V(R). The less the direct effect of location advantage on utility, the greater the increase in consumer income needed to offset the increase in rents and, consequently, the greater the shift of the V(R) curve needed to keep the maximum utility level unchanged and equal to v in equilibrium. Therefore, any region with location advantage and income combinations in quadrant A in Figure 6 is classified as "firm dominated rich" region, because the primary reason that this region's incomes, location advantage, and rents differ from those of the average region is the below-average cost effects of location advantage. This below-average cost effect is reflected in the ability of producers in these regions to pay higher average incomes and rents for having at their disposal a greater than the average location advantage, which reduces their cost.

Similarly regions with below average incomes and location advantage (quadrant C in Figure 6) are classified as "firm dominated poor" regions, because the primary reason that this region's incomes, location advantage, and rents differ from those of the average region is the above-average cost effects of location advantage.

Consumer dominated regions are reflected by quadrants B and D. These regions are associated with increases in rents and decreases in incomes reflecting the consumers' willingness to pay relatively more for the effects of the regional characteristics embodied in the region's location advantage. Quadrant B then identifies "Consumer dominated rich" regions where the location advantage is greater than the average. Similarly regions in quadrant D, are characterized as "Consumer dominated poor" regions.

EMPIRICAL SPECIFICATION AND RESULTS

As an application of the above theory, we specify the following location advantage function of a region:[1]

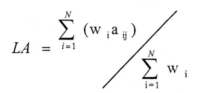

$$LA = \frac{\sum_{i=1}^{N} (w_i a_{ij})}{\sum_{i=1}^{N} w_i}$$

for j = 1, 2, 3, ..., m

where a_{ij} is the ith location characteristic of region j, w_i is the weight for the characteristic i, N is the number of location and other characteristics considered, and m is the number of regions being examined. The weights w_i can be all equal to 1/N or be assigned a-theoritically using principal component or survey results. However, in all cases the weights should be the same across regions, that is, they should not be indexed by j.

We compute the location advantage LA for EU member states, by using the following variables:

$Y_{1,j}$ Weekly hours of work (per person in manufacture)
$Y_{2,j}$ Annual leave days and holidays (days per person in manufacture),
$Y_{3,j}$ Life expectancy at birth (Years),
$Y_{4,j}$ Population per doctor,
$Y_{5,j}$ Mean years of schooling,
$Y_{6,j}$ Women in upper secondary gross enrollment ratio,
$Y_{7,j}$ Urban population (as % of total),
$Y_{8,j}$ Daily newspaper circulation,
$Y_{9,j}$ Televisions(per 1000 people),
$Y_{10,j}$ Telephones (per 1000 people),
$Y_{11,j}$ Military expenditure (as % of GDP),
$Y_{12,j}$ Public expenditure on health (as % of GDP),
$Y_{13,j}$ Social security benefits expenditure (as % of GDP),
$Y_{14,j}$ Expenditure on research and development (as % of GNP),
$Y_{15,j}$ Total education expenditure (as % of GNP),
$Y_{16,j}$ Labour force (as % of total population),
$Y_{17,j}$ Women in labour force(as % of total labour force),
$Y_{18,j}$ Population density

---

[1] Similar indices have been used in the past by Hope and Parker (1990, 1995), Hope et al (1991, 1992), Giannias (1996,1997,1998), Giannias, Liargovas and Manolas (1999) Roback (1982, 1988), Blomquist et al (1988) and Gyourko and Tracy (1991).

The above variables for each country are scaled from 0 to 100 using the following transformations:

1) $y_{ij}^* = 100\ (Y_{ij} - Y_{ijmin})/(Y_{ijmax} - Y_{ijmin})$

where, y_{ij}^* is the transformed variable, Y_{ijmin} is the minimum value of Y_{ij}, and Y_{ijmax} is the maximum value, for $i = 1, 3, 4, 5, 6, 7, 8, 9, 10, 12, 14, 15, 16, 17$, that is, for all variables having a positive relationship with LA, and all j, and

2) $y_{ij}^* = 100 - [100\ (Y_{ij} - Y_{ijmin})/(Y_{ijmax} - Y_{ijmin})]$

where, y_{ij}^* is the transformed variable, Y_{ijmin} is the minimum value of Y_{ij} in the sample of countries and Y_{ijmax} is the maximum value, $i = 2, 11, 18$, that is, for all variables having a negative relationship with LA, and all j.

Finally, to compute LA for each country we have (i) used data from the Human Development Report 1997, (ii) taken $a_{ij} = y_{ij}^*$, and (iii) The weights of the scaled variables y_{ij}^* were based on a 1996 expert's opinion survey. In this opinion survey we asked 88 regional and urban experts to value on a 0-100 scale the importance of each one of the above 18 variables for the location quality of a region. The average weights for each variable were used to compute location advantage. The weights are given in Table 2.

Table 2: Weights from Expert's Opinion Survey*

Variable	Weight
Weekly hours of work (per person in manufacture.)	71,43
Annual leave days and holidays (days per person. in manufacture)	71,43
Life expectancy at birth (Years)	90,00
Population per doctor	88,57
Mean years of schooling	82,86
Women in upper secondary gross enrollment ratio	78,57
Urban population (as % of total)	60,00
Daily newspaper circulation	80,00
Televisions (per 1000 people)	82,86
Telephones (per 1000 people)	88,57
Military expenditure (as % of GDP)	68,57
Public expenditure on health (as % of GDP)	92,86
Social security benefits expenditure (as % of GDP)	71,43
Expenditure on research and development (as % of GNP)	75,71
Total education expenditure (as % of GNP)	92,86
Labour force (as % of total pop.)	78,57
Women in labour force (as % of total labour force)	84,29
Population density	58,57

(*) 88 experts form the EU participated in this survey conducted in 1996. All these experts have been involved in economics, regional and environmental research during the last three years.

The per capita income, I, of each country is also scaled from 0 to 100 using the following transformation:

$$I_j^* = 100 \ (I_j - I_{min})/(I_{max} - I_{min})$$

where, I_j^* is the transformed index, I_{min} is the minimum index value in the sample of countries and I_{max} is the maximum value, and $j = 1, 2, 3, ..., m$.

The location advantage and per capita income combinations, (LA,I^*), for EU member states are given in Table 3. Table 3 and the results of our theoretical analysis imply the positioning mapping of Figure 8. This identifies four group of countries, namely, firm dominated rich countries: Sweden, Germany, Denmark, Finland, France and Austria, consumer dominated rich countries: Netherlands, UK, Belgium, consumer dominated poor country: Luxembourg and firm dominated poor countries: Italy, Ireland, Spain, Portugal and Greece.

Table 3: Per Capita Income and Location Advantage Function of the EU member states (Differences from the mean)

	I*	LA
AUSTRIA	2,74	0,53
BELGIUM	-20	1,13
DENMARK	14,11	10,18
FINLAND	21,05	7,12
FRANCE	4,69	7,31
GERMANY	13,85	5,5
GREECE	-40,19	-27,3
IRELAND	-25,78	-18,79
ITALY	-4,26	-12,61
LUXEMBOURG	35,82	-10,43
NETHERLANDS	-1,98	7,09
PORTUGAL	-43,69	-26,31
SPAIN	-23,66	-14,3
SWEDEN	18,54	22,22
UNITED KINGDOM	-6,91	1,2

Figure 8

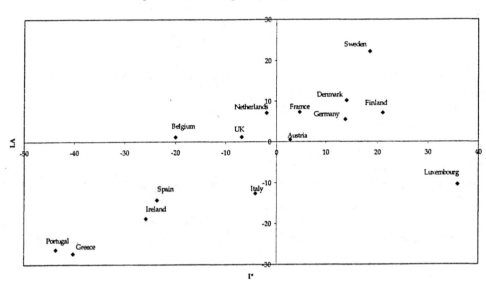

Figure 8. Location Advantages and per capita Income in the EU

CONCLUSIONS

This paper challenged the Neo-classical argument that regional inequalities are due to consumer income differentials and that under certain assumptions output (and income) of different regions should tend to converge over time towards a steady state. It built upon the argument that location advantages associated with site-specific characteristics in each region create external economies and therefore consumer income differentials can persist over time.

A theory was presented to model the effects of location and income differentials on interregional differences. Based on this theory we determined whether location and income differences primarily reflect consumers' or firms' dominated responses. In the first case we would see a negative relationship between location advantage and incomes. In the second case, the relationship would be positive. We also classified individual regions or countries on the basis of whether their incomes and location advantage differ from the average. This kind of classification is useful because it provides information about the relative attractiveness to consumers and producers of the total bundle of location and other attributes indigenous to each region.

We applied this theory in order to determine the relative importance of location advantage and income differences as sources of regional disparities across countries in the EU. The analysis showed that Italy, Ireland, Spain, Portugal and Greece could be characterized as firm dominated poor countries. Among the rest, Sweden, Germany, Denmark, Finland, France and Austria are firm dominated rich countries, Netherlands, UK and Belgium are consumer dominated rich country. Finally Luxembourg is consumer dominated poor country.

REFERENCES

1. CONLISK, J. (1969) A Neoclassical Growth Model with Endogenously Positioned Technical Change Frontier, *Economic J.* 348-62.
2. GIANNIAS, D. (1996) Quality of life in Southern Ontario, *Canadian Journal of Regional Science*, **19** (2).
3. GIANNIAS, D. (1997) Quality of Life Structural analysis, *Journal of Environmental Management*, **49**, 157-166.
4. GIANNIAS, D. (1998) A quality of Life based ranking of Canadian cities, *Urban Studies*, **35**(12).
5. GIANNIAS, D., LIARGOVAS P. AND MANOLAS G. (1999) Quality of Life Indices for Analyzing Convergence in the European Union, *Regional Studies*, **33**(1), 27-35.
6. GYOURKO, J. AND TRACY, J. (1991) The structure of local public finance and the quality of life, *Journal of Political Economy*, **99**, 774-805.
7. HOPE, C. AND J. PARKER (1990) Environmental information for all- the need for a monthly index, *Energy Policy*, **18** (4), 312-319.
8. HOPE, C., J. PARKER AND S. PEAKE (1991) A pilot index for the UK results of the last decade *Statistical Journal of the UN Economic Commission for Europe*, **8**(1), 85-107.
9. HOPE, C., J. PARKER AND S. PEAKE (1992) A pilot environmental index for the UK in the 80s *Energy Policy,* **20** (4), 335-343.
10. HOPE, C. AND J. PARKER (1995) Environmental indices for France, Italy and the UK *European Environment*, **5**(1).
11. HUMAN DEVELOPMENT REPORT, (1995, 1997, 1999), Published for the United Nations Development Programme.
12. ROBACK, J. (1988) Wages, rents and amenities: Differences among workers and regions, *Economic Inquiry*, January.
13. ROBACK, J. (1982) Wages, rents and the quality of life, *Journal of Political Economy*, **90** (6).
14. KRUGMAN, P. (1991) Increasing Returns and Economic Geography, *Journal of Political Economy* **99**(3).
15. KRUGMAN P., AND VENABLES, A. (1990) Integration and the Competitiveness of Peripheral Industry. In: C. Bliss and J. Braga de Macedo (Eds), *Unity with Diversity in the European Economy: The community's Southern Frontier,* pp.56-75. Cambridge: Cambridge University Press.

16. MYRDAL, G. (1957) Economic Theory and Underdeveloped Regions. London: Duckworth.
17. PRUD'HOMME, R. (1993) The Potential Role of the EC Budget in the Reduction of Regional Disparities in a European Economic and monetary Union. *European Economy*, Reports and Studies, 5.
18. ROBSON P. (1987) *The Economics of International Integration.* 3rd edn. London: Allen and Unwin.
19. ROMER, P.M. (1986) Increasing Returns and Long-Run Growth. *Journal of Political Economy* **98,** S71-S102.
20. SOLOW, R. M. (1956) A contribution to the Theory of Growth. *Quarterly Journal of Economics* **70,** 65-94.
21. UZAWA, H. (1965) Optimum Technical Change in an Aggregative Model of Economic Growth. *International Economic Review* **6,** 18-31.
22. UNITED NATIONS. (1997) Human Development Report. NY: Oxford University Press.
23. VAN DER PLOEG AND TANG. (1992) The Macroeconomics of Growth: An International Perspective. *Oxford Review of Economic Policy* **8**(4), 15-28.

Chapter 6

INDIVIDUAL LEARNING: EUROPEAN PERSPECTIVES

*Peter Plant**
Royal Danish School of Educational Studies, Copenhagen

In several European countries, individual learning is a current national educational strategy, both in terms of youth and adults. The article analyses this trend, it's driving forces and it's underlying value shifts.

LABELS

Under various labels, different national strategies for individual learning are being implemented in a number of European countries. The reasons for this are at least twofold. The driving forces include (1) globalisation of the market economy and the ensuing drive for labour force competitiveness, and, on the other side of the same coin, (2) the risk of social exclusion, i.e. the marginalisation of particular (low-skilled) groups in society. Together, these trends bring the issue of social inclusion via adult learning (i.e. training and education) higher up the educational agenda.

The strategies have different names which represent various aspects of the learning strategy: Individual Learning Accounts (UK), The Knowledge Uplift (Kunskapslyftet, Sweden), The National Competency Uplift (Nationalt Kompetenceløft, Denmark), and, on a more poetic note: The Joy of Learning (Lärandes Glädje, Finland), just to mention a few. Firstly, is remarkable that *education and training* are no longer in all cases current descriptions of these phenomena: *learning* is. Secondly, that something needs lifting here, and, thirdly, that learning is (should be?) a joy. Behind these catching headlines lie profound societal shifts, based on the movements of major tectonic plates of society: globalisation of the economy, the inter-linking forces of ICT, demographic changes, all

---

* *Contact address:* Dr. Peter Plant, Royal Danish School of Educational Studies, 101 Emdrupvej, DK-2400 Copenhagen NV, Denmark. Tel: + 45 39 69 66 33. Fax: + 45 39 69 74 74. E-mail: pepl@dlh.dk

resulting in careerquakes (Watts, 1996), and in the ensuing call for more flexible and, indeed, more individualised learning modes and career paths.

Thus, as the tectonic plates of society are moving, resulting in labour-market quakes and new riftlines in the educational system, education no longer mirrors the standardisation/synchronisation concept of the industrial epoch (although many schools still run on an industrial/linear/synchronised time concept, known as The Timetable, preparing students for an industrialised way of life, which is vanishing). On the contrary, in (post)modernity each individual's educational project is unique, and not always in sync with The System. It reflects the distinctive potential of each person; different from everybody else's. This process is ongoing and, in principle, lifelong: we live in times of constant reflexivity, as pointed out by Giddens (1991), where the personal educational project is interwoven with the personal project of lifelong spiritual/personal/career growth. Individually.

LEARNING

In this picture, education - or rather: *learning* - is no longer, in effect, the responsibility of institutions. It is the responsibility of creative individuals. This puts enormous pressure on each individual to be a success in their own terms, or to fail. Moreover, it puts pressure on e.g. educational institutions to be much more flexible, and ultimately break up from their present industrial-like form; its forces study grant programmes to change into support for each individual on a life-long learning basis in different countries as mentioned above (e.g. 'Individual Learning Accounts' in the UK; 'Kunskapslyftet' in Sweden); and, in terms of guidance and counselling, it requires continuous and constant personal follow-up to put together such tailorised learning programmes. These are the challenges of crossing the borders of traditional educational concepts. Politically this is highly controversial. Employers are hesitant: who, really, are these people with these individual sets of qualifications? And, inevitably, it meets some institutional resistance: flexibility is a marvellous concept, in principle, but somewhat troublesome to timetable.

On a personal, value-based level, such changes may require a revision of deeply rooted work values and overarching meta values such as: 'The Good Life'. An insight into what this might imply is offered in following sections.

VALUES AND ETHNOLOGY

Do you find yourself reading books in your spare time that might come in handy on the job? What about working through your breaks and lunch hours? Have you given any thought to how you might set up another business to make a little extra money? These are all questions that point to certain career values. The basis of this analysis of values stems from ethnology (Hojrup, 1983). Danish ethnologists during the 1980's wondered why societal planning and policy making nearly always was met with resistance by the people: the planning and policy making was conducted for the good of the people, was it not? But each time new regulations and rules were introduced, people found ways of deviating. There was always some way of getting round fishing quotas; the informal economy was often seen a way out of the neat, planned economy. But more importantly, perhaps, it was clear that a value gap existed between the policy makers and the people. Perhaps they led such different lives, based on opposing value systems that their values did not meet. What were these values? What did they see as 'The Good life'? Via in-depth interviews, mapping family and other relations, photographic recording of homes and leisure activities, and, in fact, living for extended periods of time with the people of a particular part of Northern Denmark, the ethnologists identified three sets of value systems, each one with distinct characteristics in terms of careers: *the careerist, the wage-earner, and the entrepreneur* (Christensen 1987; 1988). A brief summary is presented in Figure 1 (below):

Fig. 1: Work-Values, Leisure, and Life-Long Learning

	Work	**Leisure**	**Life-Long Learning**
Careerist	Personal development	Interwoven	Personal growth
Wage-Earner	A job	Separate	Instrumental
Entrepreneur	A task	Patchy	Instrumental

The three sets of work values, as indicated above, have little in common, and do not share each other's basic values. For two of them (careerist and entrepreneur) work and 'leisure' blends into a flow of time and effort, as opposed to the wage-earner, who wants a clear-cut distinction between the two. The careerist and the entrepreneur, in turn, do not agree on the fundamental issue of the concept of 'work'. The former feels that work constitutes an important (indeed the most important) component in personal development (as does life-long learning), whereas the latter is more instrumental in her/his approach. In short, each of the three categories are often culturally blind towards each others' sets of career values, which in the global economy are undergoing profound changes, becoming much less wage-earner and more careerist oriented (Plant, 1997). Such changes have wide implications for the educational system; the concept of the 'system' itself is under siege. Life-Long Learning is required for all three categories, but their motivation differs hugely: only for the careerist is learning linked with personal growth. They thrive on such activities. For the two other categories training will do: Life-Long Learning is a pressure from outside sources. It should be limited and instrumental. Perhaps the whole concept of Life-Long Learning was coined by careerists in the first place? Their values and preferences are dominating those of the others', once again. They define what is 'The Good Life'.

The following sections contain some selected examples of how the challenge of Life-Long Learning has been handled in three different European countries (Denmark,

Sweden, and the UK), both in terms of youth and adult education. The common emphasis on individual learning is evident in all three cases, but with a different slant.

OPEN YOUTH EDUCATION, FRI UNGDOMSUDDANNELSE, DENMARK

How does the educational 'system' react towards such changing work patterns and values: is the 'Individual Career' possible and sustainable in the present rather rigid educational systems? An example of recent developments in Denmark may serve as an illustration: transgressing the conventional borders of education, Danish Open Youth Education (Fri Ungdomsuddannelse, FUU; from 1995) redefines the concept of education altogether (Undervisningsministeriet, 1996). Over 2-3 years, individuals (no upper age-limit; most participants are in their early 20s, the oldest one is 65 years of age: eternal youth in Denmark!) plan their own route of interwoven *learning components*: training, education, work experiences, voluntary work, and the participants' own projects are all seen as learning opportunities, in each case held together by a personal learning focus, a theme. About half of the plans include study periods abroad. This is encouraged by extra funding provided for such components in addition to the normal state-funded study grants (SU) which are available for all students. Education in Denmark is free, in principle, but in the case of Open Youth Education most students find that they have extra expenses. Mostly due to their creative and imaginative learning plans. The overall guidelines are rather loose: there is no fixed curriculum, no syllabus, no exams (apart from the ones that might be embedded in parts taken from other educational options) - and no age limit.

However, some rules do apply: A two-year study period must contain at least three such components; a three-year period at least four. Most plans have many more elements: up to a dozen or so. All individual plans are recorded in a personal contract, and form part of the personal portfolio which provides the basis of subsequent credit transfer to other types of education. Societal control is administered by the personal counsellor (in most cases a teacher/counsellor in the first/starting educational institution). This is an interesting concept in terms of guidance and counselling: the very loose guidelines are in effect translated into practice by each counsellor in collaboration with the Open Youth Education participant. Some create the wildest of plans, aiming at vocations such as 'Adventure Tour Guide', 'Falconer', or 'Clown'. Others are more apprehensive. Some almost modest in their personal goal: 'I want to be able to run my own household'. All plans have an overarching theme which gives direction to each component of the individual plan. Approximately 14,000 individuals have taken part in this programme over the last 4 years; 7,000 are active just now (December, 1999). For comparison, a year cohort in Denmark is approx. 50,000 persons. About 3,000 individuals have finished their education; the drop-out rate from the programme is approx. 28% (of the 14,000), 70% of which is 'positive' drop out in the sense that the drop-outs have taken up employment in their field or other lines of study closely related to their initial FUU-plan. These figures are remarkably low compared to other dropout schemes.

The original motivation to set up Open Youth Education was the concern in the mid-1990s about an overall much too high dropout rate from Danish general and vocational (youth) education. Some official data showed that the dropout rate was probably as high as 25% in terms of persons not completing such education during this period. Potential social losers were, statistically, to be found in this group: a waste of talent and economic resources. With this backdrop, a number of preventative educational measures were established, one of which was Open Youth Education. One interesting feature in this educational policy is that Open Youth Education first and foremost initially was seen as an instrument to prevent dropout. Potential participants were consequently regarded as the weak, the social outcasts. Four years later (1999), in reality, the picture is much more varied: Open Youth Education appeals to a variety of individuals, many of whom do not see themselves as losers. On the contrary. They see Open Youth Education as their chance to realise personal plans, in many cases in terms of enhancing creative or personal pedagogical/social competencies. About half of the participants continue on further and higher education, thus, in practice, living up to the official goal of motivating the students of Open Youth Education to enter into Life-Long Learning.

Recent research has shown that the majority of participants do not have personal problems in terms of lack of self-esteem, loneliness, or even school-related difficulties (PLS-Consult, 1998; 1999). And yet, they are in fact classified as educational dropouts. The contradiction in terms is evident. What does this seem to indicate? Firstly, that policy-making does not always take the intended direction. Side effects do occur, in addition to reaching the original targets. Secondly, that young people (most of the participants are in their early 20s) are voting with their feet. They want more freedom in their education; they do not want pre-packaged sequences of education with very little room for individuality; they want to cross the borders between education, training, work, and their own projects, and mix these ingredients into new forms of personal and tailorised qualifications: gathering a portfolio of personal, individualised competencies. Indeed, the life- and learning styles of the portfolio (careerist) people are mirrored right here. Thirdly, the era of inflexible institutionalised education is drawing to an end. Instead the emphasis is on individual needs and qualifications. All such changes are crossing well-established concepts of boundaries. Sometimes to the disapprovement of the more classical/rigid educational institutions. For more information see: www.uvm.dk/eng/publications.

ADULT EDUCATION INITIATIVE, KUNSKAPSLYFTET, SWEDEN

The Swedish Adult Education Initiative, known as 'Kunskapslyftet', is a five-year programme of investment and development in adult education initiated by the Swedish government in July 1997. The programme is about boosting participants' job-related skills, and is conceived as a tool for helping the country achieve four important objectives: a renewal of policy relating to (1) the labour market, and (2) education and training; (3) a fairer distribution of wealth; and (4) increased economic growth. The principal target-group are unemployed adults without three years of upper-secondary school education (in Sweden upper secondary education to the basic level required for entrance to higher education generally covers three years). The aim is to enable people to acquire improved self-confidence, to increase their employability and to make them more able to make use of opportunities for furthering their own development in their work. The programme is designed to assist participants in achieving the necessary qualifications and competence levels to study at a higher level, and to lay the foundations for lifelong learning. It is a stated aim of the Adult Education Initiative to contribute to the development and renewal of adult education, in terms both of its content and working methods. A total of 100,000 participants per year is the official goal.

A number of basic principles support this approach (for more information see: www.kunskapslyftet.gov.se/english):

- A concerted effort to lower the threshold which inhibits those not used to studying from getting started. Among other things this entails effective efforts to bring those in need into the programme, individually tailored study plans, intensified careers counselling, and the provision of information in new forms and via new channels.
- Increased utilisation of different providers of education and training, where account is taken of the differences in the providers' profile, working methods and contact networks to ensure that they are a resource in pursuing the objectives of the Adult Education Initiative.
- The applying of new forms of activity, unconventional organisational solutions, information technology and an educational approach adapted to adults' needs and abilities.

LIFELONG LEARNING

1996 was 'Continuing Education Year' in the European Union. One of the questions which was discussed in this framework was how a strategy for continuing education, i.e. lifelong learning, might be conceived. The Ministers of Education of the OECD countries highlighted three corner-stones: a good standard of basic education as the foundation for lifelong learning; increased opportunities for switching between study and work throughout working life; and a clarification of the roles of, and the distribution of responsibility between, the different parties involved.

In the Swedish case, it is interesting to note how value-driven this approach is; how policy-driven, in fact: the curriculum which applies to all adult education (Lpf 94) lays down the value-base and tasks of adult education. For example, the specified targets of adult education include:

- Reducing discrepancies in the level of education and training between individuals, thus contributing to greater equality and social justice;

- Enabling students to increase their ability to understand, judge and participate in cultural, social and political life, thus contributing to democratic development in society;
- Providing adults with training and education which equips them to carry out varying work tasks; the programme is also to provide an input to the process of change in the conditions of working life, and is to make a contribution to the effort to attain full employment, thus promoting development and progress in society;
- Meeting the wishes expressed by individuals for expanded study and training opportunities, and making it possible for them to supplement the basic school education they had as children.

The curriculum is given more precise, concrete expression in the form of syllabuses for each subject. The syllabuses lay down what the objectives for each course are, and also what skills and knowledge students are expected to have attained on completion of the course. In these terms, the Swedish top-down individual learning approach is more prescriptive than for example the Danish one. For more information see: www.skolverket.se/skolnet.

The next section depicts a both contrasting and complementary English example, ILA (Individual Learning Accounts) which in terms of the policy rhetoric is a far cry from the Swedish approach, but in practice has many similarities in terms of e.g. diversity in delivery and the focus on individual learning.

INDIVIDUAL LEARNING ACCOUNTS (ILA), UK

'INDIVIDUAL LEARNING ACCOUNTS GO FULL STEAM AHEAD FOR 2000', headlines established in May 1999, citing Education and Employment Secretary David Blunkett, UK, in his comments on a report on the progress and development of individual learning accounts. He further 'Pledged to put the individual at the heart of the learning revolution when the full rollout of accounts happens nationwide next year. A report (A Summary of Progress on Individual Learning Accounts) had found that:

'People welcomed individual learning accounts as a means of overcoming cost, one of the main barriers to learning.....more accessible accounts would help and support a change in career direction'.

'The accounts will pave the way for more learning and more effective learning and the wider philosophy, that the more you learn, the more you earn. This is evident from the learning account pilot projects already being run,' said the Secretary, adding that: 'People make a difference in the wealth creation process and learning is a key agent to help. For a small contribution from the individual, the Government will put in £150 to the first million accounts and offer large discounts of 80 per cent for certain courses and 20 per cent for others. An individual learning account will be a special bank account to help individuals plan and pay for learning. Accounts should add value to existing employer investment, currently running at over £10 billion a year for training and development. Today's report also underlines the interest in Individual Learning Accounts from small businesses whose level of investment in learning is generally lower than larger firms. The accounts will help the smaller firms catch up.'

To provide a further insight into the UK rhetoric on individual learning with a heavy emphasis on the market-economy based approach, the following sections contain some extracts of the ILA homepage (for more information see: www.lifelonglearning.co.uk/ila):

'What is an individual learning account?
An individual learning account will offer a facility for you to save money to pay for your own learning (e.g. an evening class at your local college). The account will be owned by you, and subject to some conditions, will attract some form of public contribution.

Who can open an individual learning account?
Accounts will be available to everyone. Up to the first million people who open an account - available to anyone in the world of work but not in full-time education - will qualify for a £150 contribution from their local Training and Enterprise Council (TEC), provided they contribute at least £25 of their own money and spend the money on eligible learning which is relevant to their current employment or to jobs they want to do.

Is an individual learning account like a bank account?
The Government hopes that, in time, learning accounts will be offered in a similar way to other bank accounts. For now, your local TEC will make its own arrangements to provide the £150 of support to those who qualify for it. In some areas, TECs are working with banks to provide the account, but in most areas other arrangements will be in place during 1999.

If my employer contributes to my learning, will I have to pay tax on this?
From next year, employers will be able to contribute to individual learning accounts tax free, provided they contribute to those of the lowest paid employees on similar terms. If your employer contributes, that money will be tax free if it is used for agreed learning. There will need to be safeguards to ensure employer contributions are only used to pay for agreed learning.

Where can I get help/advice with learning now?
The national freephone helpline Learning Direct provides up-to-date, confidential advice on learning and courses to suit your needs, and can refer you to local advice services and education providers. The number is 0800 100 900.'

Evidently, individual learning needs individual guidance with free-phone facilities. But the fascinating feature in the quoted piece is the market-oriented jargon. Here the learner is spending her/his own money, shopping for the best option in the Learning Supermarket. Being individually marketable in terms of employability is the ultimate aim. This aim may also be read between the lines in the Danish and Swedish cases. But the latter, in particular, in addition features aims such as 'To enable students to increase their ability to understand, judge and participate in cultural, social and political life, thus contributing to democratic development in society', as mentioned above. The difference in terminology is linked with current policies and historical background: the market-economy language stems from the belief that Adam Smith's Invisible Hand will create a balance between supply and demand (here: educationally), whereas the democracy-focused approach in Sweden dates back 150 years to the 'people's enlightenment' movement: adult education is one of its foundation stones. Interestingly, both approaches end up with similar solutions with a strong focus on individual learning. Why? Because individuals and their personal capacities/creativity and eagerness to pursue life-long learning are pivotal in modern working life. The values of the careerist are manifest.

Prof. Peter Plant, M.Ed., Ph.D., trains school and employment counsellors, and works in European research teams on adult education and career development. Vice-President of the International Association for Educational and Vocational Guidance (IAEVG).

REFERENCES

1. Christensen, L.B. (1987): Arbejdsbegreber, familietyper og born i tre forskellige livsformer. In: Plant, P. (1987): *Fremtider. Fredensborg: Studie og Erhverv.*
2. Christensen, L.B. (1988): *Livsformer i Danmark.* Copenhagen: Samfundsfagsnyt.
3. Giddens, A. (1991): *Modernity and Self-Identity.* Cambridge: Polity Press.
4. Hojrup, Th. (1983): *Det glemte folk.* Horsholm: Statens Byggeforskningsinstitut.
5. Plant, P. (1997): Work values and counselling: Careerist, wage-earner or entrepreneur (in) *International Journal for the Advancement of Counselling,* Vol. 19, 1997. Dordrecht: Kluwer Academic Publishers.
6. Plant, P. & Romer, L. (1991): *Arbejdsvaerdier.* Copenhagen: Dansk Arbejdsgiverforening.
7. PLS-Consult (1998; 1999): *Evaluering af den Fri Ungdomsuddannelse.* Aarhus: PLS-Consult.
8. Undervisningsministeriet (1996): *Open Youth Education.* Copenhagen: Danish Ministry of Education. Pamphlet in English; available in German and French.
9. Watts, A.G. (1996): *Careerquake.* London: Demos.

Chapter 7

THE COMMON AGRICULTURAL POLICY: PAST, PRESENT AND FUTURE*

Nicholas C. Baltas

Professor of Economics & Holder of Jean Monnet Chair
Department of Economics, Athens University of Economics and Business

ABSTRACT

When the EC countries decided to tackle in common the agricultural problem by setting up a Common Agricultural Policy (CAP) they embarked on a task of immense economic and social implications. Despite the difficulties which this has caused from the start, many observers agree that on the whole the EC has succeeded in establishing its most comprehensive common policy.

The main purpose of this short analysis is to present an overview of the main developments of the CAP and to outline its prospects beyond the turn of the century taking into account the enlargement of the European Union and the negotiations with the World Trade Organisation (WTO). The EU's negotiating position in future WTO negotiations will be formulated along the lines of the Berlin agreement, which fall far short of the US objectives regarding the liberalization of the international trade in agricultural commodities. Moreover, a delay is expected in EU's eastward enlargement. Nevertheless, over the next seven years, it will be the first time in the EU's history that spending on agriculture will not have shown constant growth in real terms. The agreement also recognizes that agriculture contributes to the preservation of natural resources and the European heritage and maintains the visual amenity of the countryside. Finally, it seeks to respond to consumer concerns on food safety, quality and animal welfare issues.

---

* The grant provided by the European Commission is thankfully acknowledged.

INTRODUCTION

When the EC countries decided to tackle in common the agricultural problem by setting up a Common Agricultural Policy (CAP) they embarked on a task of immense economic and social implications. Despite the difficulties which this has caused from the start, many observers agree that on the whole the EC has succeeded in establishing its most comprehensive common policy. The CAP, in a way, still reflects the balance of interests and the compromises reached between the six original Community members, which continue to have vested social and economic interests in their agricultural sectors.

The main purpose of this short analysis is to present an overview of the main developments of the CAP and to outline its prospects beyond the turn of the century taking into account the enlargement of the European Union and the negotiations with the World Trade Organisation (WTO).

OBJECTIVES AND PRINCIPLES OF THE CAP

The main objectives of the CAP are clearly defined in Article 39 of the Treaty of Rome as follows:

- to increase agricultural productivity by promoting technical progress;
- thus to ensure a fair standard of living for the agricultural community;
- to stabilise markets;
- to assure the availability of supplies;
- to ensure that supplies reach consumers at reasonable prices.

The CAP was set up on three principles which guide every policy: the single market, community preference and financial solidarity.

AN EVALUATION OF THE COMMON AGRICULTURAL POLICY

The CAP was created at a time when Europe was in deficit for most food products. Its mechanisms were devised to meet this situation. In essence, they support internal prices and incomes, either through intervention or border protection or, where no frontier protection exists, by variable aids in the form of deficiency payments.

The main policy instrument before the 1992 reform of the CAP was price support. This was adopted not because it was considered to be the most efficient means of achieving the set objectives but because it is generally regarded as less interventionist than other policies, such as direct subsidies, and therefore politically more acceptable to the taxpayer.

The original CAP system revealed a number of advantages but also some serious deficiencies:

- Community prices of agricultural products are more stable than world prices, though at significantly higher levels.
- The CAP ensured security of supply of agricultural products in the Community through increased self-sufficiency.
- Intra-Community trade of agricultural products multiplied manyfold.
- Labour productivity in agriculture grew by more than 6 per cent a year, while the corresponding percentage for average labour productivity in the Community was about 4 per cent.
- High prices and guarantees stimulated output increases which went beyond the market's absorptive capacity. Between 1973 and 1991, the volume of agricultural production in the EC increased by 2 per cent per annum whereas internal consumption grew by only 0.5 per cent per annum. This resulted in surpluses for some commodities. In the 1991 budget, these stocks were worth 3.7 billion ECU.
- The impressive rise in agricultural output has led to a spectacular increase in Community expenditure[1] on price support. The budget of the Guarantee Section rose from 4.5 billion ECU in 1975 to 11.5 billion ECU in 1991 at constant 1975 prices. Although European Agricultural Guidance and Guarantee Fund (EAGGF) expenditure increased over this twenty-year period approximately twice as fast as the rate of growth of Community GDP, real farm incomes remained almost unchanged. Three explanations of this paradox were offered: it was argued that, first, most incomes in the economy experienced stagnation or decline and that without the support of the CAP a fall in farm incomes would have been inevitable; second, the price support policy was not an efficient method for raising incomes; and third, half of the Guarantee Section expenditure is accounted for by the cost of stocking surpluses and by export restitutions.
- The public cost of protection of the agricultural markets seemed to increase inexorably, limiting the funds available for other purposes.
- Since the system linked agricultural support with quantities produced, it inevitably stimulated production growth and thus encouraged intensification of production techniques and use of more farm inputs.
- A consequence of the price support policy was that the largest and the most intensive farms absorbed the greater part of EAGGF funds. It was calculated that 80 per cent of the support provided by EAGGF was directed to just 20 per cent of farms.

---

[1] The Commission noted in 1981 that agriculture spending was growing faster than the growth of the Community's budgetary resources. Having reached 68 per cent of total spending in 1985, the burden of the CAP has since declined below 50 per cent of the budget. This happened as the Commission managed to control spending of the CAP especially as to reflect the diminishing share of the agricultural sector of the overall economy. Since 1988 the annual rate of increase of the "agricultural budget guideline" has been limited to 74 per cent of the growth (nominal increase) of the EU GDP. The decline in agriculture's relative budgetary importance has been accompanied by a market increase in the proportion of the budget dedicated to the Structural Funds.

- EAGGF expenditure was traditionally dominated by the support provided to the "northern commodities" (i.e. milk, sugar, beef and veal) which received above-average protection. The "southern commodities" (i.e. fruit, vegetables, olive oil, cotton, wine, sheep and goat meat and tobacco) have traditionally played a minor role in the history, and certainly in the cost, of the CAP.

- World market prices for most agricultural products were well below those of the EC. Hence, the European consumer lost from having to pay very high prices. Moreover, as the poor in the population spend a relatively higher proportion of their disposable income on food and the CAP's price support mechanism keeps food prices high, the CAP causes massive transfers of income from consumers in one member country to producers in another.

- Under the CAP, the European Community has changed from net importer to net exporter of food and agricultural products. This turnaround has been the outcome of support policies rather than of any market-created shift in comparative advantage. In its trading capacity, the EC has been accused of using protectionism as an instrument for social policy in support of farmers and of adding to the instability of world markets by buying agricultural products abroad only when domestic supplies are short and by selling its surpluses on world markets at subsidised prices. This has not only caused serious financial problems to the Community but also to its major trading partners and to the less developed countries and has complicated EU international relations.[2]

REFORM OF THE CAP AND ITS CONSEQUENCES ON THE EU

On 21 May 1992, the Council of Ministers reached political agreement on far-reaching changes to the CAP. Although the reform makes fairly wide-ranging changes to the rules in force until then, it does not invalidate the objectives laid down in Article 39 of the EEC Treaty or the three principles on which the CAP was founded. The basic policy instruments, i.e. intervention buying to support market prices and variable levies and export refunds to close the gap between Community and world market prices, have been kept in place, albeit at much lower levels. In addition, they have been supplemented by new instruments (Swinbank, 1993), namely:

- a substantial reduction in the prices of agricultural products to make them more competitive both within the Community and on world markets;
- compensation for the price cuts in the form of hectare or headage payments;
- implementation of measures to limit the use of factors of production (set-aside of arable land and stocking rate criteria) alongside the retention of earlier supply management measures such as the milk production quotas;

---

[2] It should be emphasized that the EU is not just the world's second-largest exporter of agricultural goods, it is also the biggest importer.

- introduction of accompanying measures such as environmentally friendly farming, afforestation and early retirement of farmers.

The reform regarding farm incomes support implies a major shift in emphasis from price support to the use of a mixed system of lower prices supplemented by compensation payments. It covers 75 per cent of agricultural production falling under common market organisations.

For cereals, the support price was lowered by about 30 per cent, bringing it close to world market levels. Producers was compensated for the price cut in the form of hectare payments. To be eligible for these compensatory payments, the larger producers (with a production capacity of 92 tonnes of cereals or more) had to set aside 15 per cent of their arable land, while small farmers were exempted. The same policy was adopted for oil-seeds.

In the milk sector, the butter intervention price was reduced by 5 per cent over two years. The quota system was maintained, although the reference quantity could be cut by a further 2 per cent spread over two years. Greece and Spain received a quota increase of 100,000 and 500,000 tonnes respectively in order to make up part of their serious deficit in fresh milk output.

In the beef sector, the intervention price was reduced by 15 per cent and a headage payment was introduced to make up for the drop. In the sheep sector, a limit per producer of a 1000 head in the less favoured areas and of 500 elsewhere was introduced for the number of ewes eligible for the premium.

For tobacco, the varieties produced in the Community were regrouped into 5 categories plus 3 special varieties of Greek tobacco. The global maximum quantity eligible for a premium was reduced from 370,000 tonnes in 1993 to 350,000 tonnes in the 1994-95 period and intervention and export refunds were discontinued.

The agri-environmental measures were directed at promoting environmentally friendly production methods for which farmers would receive extra aids in recognition of their role in the protection of the rural environment and management of the countryside. Against a background of Community deficits in wood and wood products and in recognition of the environmental importance of woodland, the afforestation programme was meant to provide additional finance for planting trees on agricultural land no longer needed for productive purposes. Finally, the early retirement scheme was intended to increase the aids available to older farmers wishing to step out, on condition that the land released be used to improve the production structure and economic viability of the remaining farm holdings.

After the 1992 reform, there has been considerable improvement in market imbalances and a decrease of public stocks in most of the reformed sectors. The general evolution of agricultural per capita incomes has been positive since the reform, growing on average by 4.5 per cent yearly between 1992 and 1996, with a diversity of situations according to member states and farm orientations. Favourable market conditions, the strong adaptative capacity of farmers, the agri-monetary context and, last but not least, the continuing decline in agricultural employment have contributed to this result (Baltas, 1997).

Total cereal production dropped by about 3.5 per cent in the three years following the reform. One of the major contributory causes to this cut-back in production was, undoubtedly, the success of the set-aside programme, introduced as an integral part of the whole reform process.[3] Under the reformed CAP, the intervention price for all cereals was reduced, reaching 119.1 ECU per tonne in the final year of the reform. These reductions were not fully offset by compensatory payments, which reached 54.34 ECU per tonne per ha. However, the drop in production resulted in a balanced internal cereals market in which the prices that prevailed were higher than the intervention prices and thus farmers from all countries benefited in the early years of reform, especially those in the peripheral countries who were also able to take advantage of devaluing currencies to raise nominal support prices during this period. It is expected that the areas devoted to the cultivation of these crops and to set-aside will stabilize at a level of about 53.5 million hectares. Under the present policy framework, cereal production is expected to rise from 201 million tonnes in 1996 to 214 by 2005. Cereal consumption is also forecast to increase further, though at a lower rate, in response to the development of wheat production. It would be possible to react to the new cereals surpluses by increasing the compulsory set-aside rate but since EU prices remain above world prices the Union could well fail to benefit from the positive development expected on the world market.

In the case of oilseeds, too, for most of the time actual market prices have been significantly higher that the reference price, so that producers have benefited from the change in four years out of five. The Commission's intention is to remove the area restriction imposed by the Uruguay Round Agreement. Oilseed production is expected to decline between 1996 and 2006. Trade deficits in oilseeds and oilseed meals would remain at very substantial levels.

The current EU situation in the market for milk and dairy products seems fairly balanced after the CAP reform. It should, however, be underlined that market stability is still fragile and cloaks a structural surplus which consistently requires large-scale intervention in the form of subsidised end-uses.[4] Global milk demand is expected to decline by 3.1 per cent (112.2 million tonnes to 108.7) between 1995 and 2005. This is the result of decreasing consumption of some dairy products, notably butter, and

---

[3] The area devoted to cereals stood at around 36 million ha following the decision taken by the Council of Ministers to reduce set-aside by 3 percentage points in the 1995/96 marketing year. Equally significant was the fact that the first two years have not seen the increase in yield which would offset any reduction in the area under cereals. However, in the third year, the fall in yields in Spain and Portugal, due to bad weather conditions, was partially compensated for by a rise in yields in other member States, particularly in Northern Europe.

[4] The intervention price for butter was further reduced by 3 per cent as from July 1994 in order to improve its competitiveness following earlier price cuts in 1993. As a result, the target price for milk fell by 1.5 per cent. These moves have been accompanied by a drop in butter production and a sharp fall in the intervention stocks of butter and skimmed-milk powder which now stand at historically low levels. Total milk production is forecast to decline from 121.6 million tonnes 1996 to 118.1 in 2005, if the milk quotas remain unchanged over the coming years.

increasing demand for other products, such as cheese and fresh products. Further export growth in the cheese sector would appear to be constrained by WTO limitations on subsidised exports. Intervention stocks of skimmed milk powder tend to increase from 1998 onwards and will reach some 200,000 by about 2005, as the WTO export commitments become binding. For butter, WTO export commitments provide a sufficient margin for subsidised exports, so that no accumulation of intervention stocks would normally be expected.

The effects of the reform on the beef sector are similar to those on the milk sector. Here, too, intervention prices[5] for beef and veal were repeatedly reduced. These institutional price reductions were passed on to market prices, which were around 80 per cent of the prevailing intervention prices. However, the reduction in the beef intervention price was outweighed by the reduction in feeding cost and the premia on bovine animals. The favourable market situation regarding intervention stocks, which were diminishing rapidly, remained until the outbreak of the BSE crisis in March 1996. Beef production will be influenced on the one hand by the short term measures adopted in 1996 and on the other hand by the elimination of adult cattle over 30 months from the food and feed chain in the UK. Beef consumption is expected to gradually recover from the 1996 shock and return to its long-term declining trend. After 2001, if the market policy remains unchanged, production should return to its full potential with consumption continuing its long-term decline. Intervention stocks will tend to accumulate again and could reach some 1.5 million tonnes by 2005. In this case, it is not acceptable to solve the problem of over-production in the sector by the slaughtering or young calves a few days after birth. Nor can the surplus problem be solved efficiently by pure management (quotas on animal numbers or on production), as this would present major administrative complications.

In the sheep-goat sector, the Union is only 82 per cent self-sufficient. About 43 per cent of production is located in the southern countries of the EU and 5 per cent in Ireland. The basic support mechanism involves a sheep-goat premium. With the reform, the Union tried to stabilize the existing level of production in the sector which has in fact registered successive drops in the early 1990s and remained stable in 1995. In any case, no significant changes have taken place in the level of output and farm incomes.

In the case of tobacco, where more than 90 per cent of EU production is located in the four Mediterranean countries (including Italy), the 17 per cent drop of 1993 raw tobacco output in relation to 1992 is the direct result of the first-time application of the reform adopted in mid - 1992. Obviously, this measure negatively affected farm incomes. Greek farmers especially suffered significant losses because of the country's relatively large tobacco production (a little less than half of total EU output). This reduction is significant for certain varieties such as flue-cured tobacco produced in Greece.[6] Moreover, since tobacco production is localised and is one of the most labour intensive

---

[5] In fact, they were reduced by 6.2 per cent at the beginning of July 1993 and by a further 5.3 per cent at the beginning of July 1994. Two further reductions by 5 per cent each have also taken place since then, as provided for in the 1992 reform.

[6] This fell from 71,526 tonnes in 1992 to 37,921 tonnes in 1993 (i.e., a reduction of 47 per cent).

crops, net per cent farm income losses in some regions were much larger than average (Baltas, 1998).

The reform effects on the environment[7] are mixed. Some positive elements can be identified: the more rational use of fertilizer and pesticides resulting from reference price decreases, the possible environmental benefits of set-aside (if well managed), incentives for a long-term improvement in the territorial distribution of livestock rearing. In this context, it is not without interest to note that the agro-chemical industry reports reduced purchases of fertilisers and pesticides by farmers. But there are also negative elements, mainly the encouragement given to irrigated crops through the regionalization of direct payments to cereals, oilseeds and protein crops, as well as the relative advantage given to intensive livestock farming through lower feed prices and subsidized silage.

The plans on afforestation influence mostly the northern farmers, as farm sizes in the south are typically too small to be suitable for afforestation. Regulation (EEC) No.2080/92 institutes a Community aid scheme for forestry measures in agriculture.

Conversely, the early retirement scheme instituted by Regulation (EEC) No. 2079/92 might be particularly beneficial in the periphery of the EU, since in the South nearly three fifths of the farmers are over the age of 55 while in Ireland less than half are above this age. The resulting restructuring of farm holdings will create the necessary conditions for maintaining the maximum number of viable farm households in the wider rural economy. Moreover, this scheme, which is co-financed by the EU, is characterized by higher levels of aid and greater flexibility in comparison to previous schemes. Although it is not compulsory, it could potentially prove very important from the social equity and macroeconomic perspectives, given the inadequate pension systems of these countries and their mounting budgetary expenditure on social security and pensions.

By 1995, nine member States (with the exception of the United Kingdom, the Netherlands and Luxembourg) had presented draft schemes for early retirement from farming. Taken together, the programmes' objective was the retirement of 184,200 farmers and 7,500 farm workers over the next six years. The area released should amount to almost 3 million ha. It is estimated that around 5 per cent of this land will be used for non-agricultural purposes, such as forestry and the creation of ecological reserves. The remainder of the area released will be taken over by other farmers, who will use it either to expand their holdings or to set up as full-time farmers.

The reduction of price support coupled with direct compensatory payments have shifted the burden of agricultural support from the consumer to the general tax-payer. Increases in the CAP budget come basically from the compensatory payments to cereal, milk and beef producers (Baltas, 1997). The overall budgetary cost in the tobacco, wine,

---

[7] Most of the 158 programmes submitted by the member States under Regulation (EEC) No. 2078/92 have been approved by the Commission. The measures under this Regulation are co-financed from the EU total budget, which provides 50 per cent of the payments for all areas and 75 per cent of the payments in Objective 1 areas (i.e. currently most of the Mediterranean countries, Ireland, the eastern Lander of Germany, and the Highlands of Scotland). This Regulation continues and extends the measures provided for in Article 19 of Regulation (EEC) No. 2328/91, which came into force before the reform of the CAP. The programmes submitted by the member States set out a variety of approaches to solving environmental problems in agriculture.

olive oil and sheep-meat sectors will decline. The benefits to consumers resulting from the reformed CAP are rather small but have marked distributional effects for the relatively poorer countries of the EU given that their consumers spend a considerably larger proportion of their disposable income on food than those in the richer ones.

THE GATT URUGUAY ROUND AGREEMENT AND THE WTO NEGOTIATIONS

The 1992 reform both anticipated and facilitated the changes brought about by the GATT Uruguay Round agreement which was concluded in 1994, came into effect July 1995 and will last until June 30, 2001. The Uruguay Round is the first-ever global trade agreement to encompass agricultural products and should bring a significant degree of liberalisation to world agricultural markets. The GATT agreement[8] on agriculture imposes disciplines on member countries in three separate areas; domestic support, market access, and export subsidies below the reference figures for 1986-88.

Domestic support

Domestic subsidies to the agricultural sector were to be reduced by 20 per cent over six years (13.3 per cent in developing countries). For the European Union, this part of the agreement has never been an issue because the various reforms of the CAP are already reducing subsidies by more than 20 per cent. The Aggregate Measure of Support (AMS) for the EU, already below the commitment for the year 2000, was further reduced by the Berlin Agreement.

Market access

All import restrictions were converted to customs tariffs (by "tariffication"). These tariffs are reduced by 36 per cent over a period of 6 years with a minimum reduction of 15 per cent for each agricultural product. For developing countries, the reduction will be by 24 per cent over 10 years, using the 1986-1988 period as base for the calculations. However, it would be wrong to think of the Uruguay Round as opening up markets and moving far toward free trade. The degree of discretion allowed to each country in their conversion procedure for non-tariff barriers led countries to set their bound tariffs somewhat higher than necessary. This was exacerbated by the fact that for many commodities the base protection rates (internal price less world price expressed as a

---

[8] For more details see e.g. Delmore and Clerc, 1994; Josling, 1994; OECD, 1995; Swinbank and Ritson, 1995.

percentage of world prices) were historically high. As a result, some of the tariffs that emerged from the Round are so high[9] as to preclude trade under normal circumstances.

Export subsidies

The volume of subsidised exports was to be reduced by 21 per cent (14 per cent for developing countries) over six years (base period 1986-90). Budgetary expenditure on export subsidies will simultaneously have to be reduced by 36 per cent - 24 per cent for developing countries over six years. Taking into account these commitments on export subsidies[10], non-exportable surpluses are likely to emerge after 2000 causing problems to the Union.

New multilateral trade negotiations formally started in December 1999 as a follow-up to the Uruguay Round, but in the end failed even to agree a negotiating agenda. Cutting border protection, reducing export subsidies and reshaping internal support towards more "decoupled" instruments will enhance the Union's regotiating stance in the new Round. On September 27 1999, the Agriculture Council unanimously adopted an aggressive approach to defend the European model of agriculture on the basis of Agenda 2000 decisions. As we will see in part 7, the Berlin Summit CAP reform outlines the EU's intentions[11] in respect of the WTO negotiations. These are rather limited compared to the ambitious U.S. objectives. In particular, the U.S. aims at the elimination of export subsidies, substantial cuts and, where possible, elimination of tariffs on farm products, reduced domestic subsidies, reform of State trading enterprises, whose monopolistic position in domestic markets distorts trade, and tightened rules on technical barriers that unjustifiably restrict trade.

On market access, the EU is going to be unreceptive toward any sweeping cuts in tariffs. A modest across-the-board reduction in tariffs is likely to be the preferred outcome, because the EU cannot move too far from its traditional protection of the domestic market. Moreover, the EU will be vulnerable on the issues of the widespread use of specific tariffs, the use of reference prices on fruit and vegetables and the high degree of excess protection for cereals as afforded by the bound tariff relative to the

---

[9] For the EU, these bound tariff rates were set at 250 per cent for sugar, 237 per cent for beef, 341 per cent for butter, and between 150 per cent and 170 per cent for grains (Harvey, 1997). CAP reform had reduced cereal prices and hence costs, whereas border protection was still reflecting the pre-reform situation. For a few commodities, those where the tariff was based on the base period grain levies (pigs, poultry and eggs), the level of protection actually rose as a result of the Uruguay Round.

[10] In the markets for coarse grains, dairy products, olive oil, beef, poultry and fresh and processed fruit and vegetables, export subsidies nave been limited as a result of the WTO constraints (Tangermann, 1999). In the case of export subsidies for wheat have been unnecessary because the EU ran down surplus from 1993 to 1996 and then in 1995 and 1996 sold wheat without subsidies onto a high-price world market.

[11] As stated in the conclusions to the European Council in Berlin on Agenda 2000: "the decisions adopted regarding the reform of the CAP within the framework of Agenda 2000 will constitute essential elements in defining the Commision's negotiating mandate for the future multilateral trade negotiations at the WTO".

"maximum duty-paid import price" for cereals which was agreed in the Uruguay Round (Josling and Babinard, 1999).

On export subsidies, the EU is likely to agree that these are essential to the clearing of markets, at least for the next few years. The Commission would rather not have to use them as instruments of policy, but it would be unacceptable to lose market share too rapidly in the cereals and dairy markets as a result of not being able to offer lower prices.

One of the most contentious issues will be the "size" and "composition" of the green box representing a possible solution to the dilemma of how one satisfies political imperatives for the maintenance of farm incomes and at the same time how one lives within the constraints of the WTO. Payments aimed at compensating farmers for the "multifunctionality" of European agriculture would be allowed even if not totally consistent with current definitions of trade-neutral instruments (Josling and Babinard, 1999).

On the blue box, the EU is likely to defend it in the early stages but could change its own compensation policies without too much inconvenience to make them compatible with the green box. If the compensation payments are not made "green", then the EU will want to maintain the "blue box" because reforms will result in increased payments for beef and cereals and the introduction of "semi-decoupled" direct payments in the dairy sector (Josling and Babinared, 1999).

Last, since CAP reform was decided before the next round of WTO negotiations, the changes adopted will clearly reflect the international constraints on the EU and will strengthen the EU in the WTO round (Coleman and Tangermann, 1999).

THE EU'S ENLARGEMENT AND THE CAP

This part of the paper considers the economic dimension of the forthcoming enlargement of the EU with regard to agriculture. Ten countries with economies in transition (Bulgaria, the Czech Republic, Estonia, Hungary, Latvia, Lithuania, Poland, Romania, Slovakia and Slovenia), and two market economies (Cyprus and Malta) negotiate full membership with the EU. Turkey became a candidate country and will have to carry out political reforms before proceeding further in the accession process. While there is no question about Cyprus and Malta being market economies (one of the conditions for the EU membership), there are still certain concerns about the acceding countries whose economies are in the long transition process. Chief among them are the increasingly demanding standards that come from the ever-growing *acquis communautaire* which are costly to introduce, implement and enforce (Jovanovic, 2000).

The entry of the thirteen countries (including Turkey) would increase the EU population by 45 per cent but its GDP by only by 6.7 per cent at current 1999 prices and by 15.8 per cent in terms of purchasing power standard (PPS) (Eurostat, 2000). As for the level of development measured by GDP per capita in PPS, the acceding countries are at a significantly lower level of development than the EU average.

The beginning of the millennium will see the eastern enlargement of the EU to include countries that until recently were command economies. Political changes in the late 1980s and early 1990s mark the beginning of important economic reforms in these countries. Initially, the main objective was to return to a market economy but soon EU accession was added to the agenda. Most countries have applied for membership and have, as a first step, become associated with the EU by agreements involving trade concessions as well as assistance to harmonize legislation, develop democratic institutions and put a market economy in place.

The reforms of 1990-1992, designed to transform the Central and Eastern European Countries (CEECs) from centrally planned to market economies, have undoubtedly obscured the true agricultural potential of the region. The liberalization of prices, production, and trade that resulted from abandoning central planning caused a sharp contraction in income and led to a fall in consumption of most foods, especially meat. Falling demand, combined with input prices rising much faster than output prices (input prices have tended to move to world market levels while agricultural output prices have tended to stagnate or rise much less in the face of falling demand) resulted in lower output. While there have been some signs of recovery since 1993-1994, particularly in the crop sector, agricultural output in most candidate countries is still well below pre-transition levels. The slow recovery is mainly due to major initial structural handicaps such as unsettled property rights, capital constraints and inefficient downstream sectors (Josling and Babinard, 1999). An important consequence of the CEECs market reforms has been a deterioration of the balance of trade between the CEECs and the EU. The significant drop in agricultural output has reduced exports to the EU, which for many candidate countries is the most important agri-food trading partner. At the same time, their agricultural imports from the EU have grown significantly after the reforms. The CEECs' growing imports from the EU are partly due to shifting consumer preferences in the region towards products such as tropical commodities and western-style processed foods (Buckwell and Tangermann, 1997). The growing trade imbalance is also caused by the pronounced differences in protection rates that exist between the CEECs and the EU.

The EU's eastward enlargement will add over 100 million consumers. Their average purchasing power, however, will be only about one third of that of consumers in the Union. On average, over 22 per cent of the workforce in the CEECs is employed in agriculture for a total of 9.5 million workers compared to 5 per cent or 8.2 million in the EU. Thus, enlargement will at least double the EU's agricultural labour force. The Union's agricultural area will increase by 60 million hectares (ha) to close to 200 million ha. Of the 60 million ha, two thirds will be arable land, adding 55 per cent to the EU's existing arable area of 77 million ha. In the CEECs, the share of agriculture in GDP ranges from 4.5 to 21 per cent compared to 2.4 per cent for the EU (EC, 1998). The CEECs have a serious need for structural improvement in their agricultural and up- and downstream sectors (Mergos, 1998). Restructuring can be expected to reduce agriculture's labour absorption capacity, implying a need for diversification of their rural economies.

Concerning the budgetary implications of the enlargement, various estimates have been made, ranging from 5 to 50 billion ECU depending on the assumptions used to develop alternative scenarios. According to EU estimates (EC, 1995), the cost of enlargement will require a 25 per cent increase of the CAP budget, which stands at 36 billion ECU. Despite these initial high estimates, the Berlin Summit agreed to set aside a budget for this future enlargement rising from Euro 6.45 billion in 2002 to Euro 16.78 billion in 2006 (Table 1). This assumes (very optimistically) that enlargement may begin from 2002. Agricultural spending will play a limited role, rising from Euro 1.6 billion in 2002 to Euro 3.4 billion in 2006.

Table 1: EU budget resource available for accession (appropriations for payments) (in million Euros, 1999 prices)

	2002	2003	2004	2005	2006
Payment appropriations	6450	9030	11610	14200	16780
Agriculture	1600	2030	2450	2930	3400
Other expenditure	4850	7000	9160	11270	13380

Source: Chairmanship's Conclusions, 24 and March 1999, Berlin.

Eastward enlargement of the EU will require extending CAP price support to new members.[12] It is generally assumed that this will involve a significant increase in producer prices in the new member states, taking into consideration that farm gate prices in the CEECs were 40 to 80 per cent of the EU level. These gaps[13] were considerably reduced but not eliminated after the Agreement on Agenda 2000. In any case is not possible at this stage, for the applicant countries to be immediately integrated in the CAP for the following reasons: First, it will trigger large supply responses in the new EU member states, in particular for sugar, milk and meat; Second, it will reduce competitiveness in the food industries of the acceding countries; and third, it will occasion sudden and undesirable changes to consumer prices resulting in a substantial reduction of consumers' real incomes, taking into consideration that households in the CEECs spend on average a relatively high proportion -30 to 60 per cent- of their disposable income on farm products.

---

[12] Whether CEECs farmers need compensation even though they are not supposed to suffer a loss of income in acceding to the CAP is a topic of much debate. Since CEECs farmers will enjoy a price rise on accession, and not a fall it has been argued that compensation is unjustified (Brittan, 1999). On the other hand, excluding new members from compensations that benefit the rest of the EU members might be inconsistent with the principle of *acquis communautaire*. Most likely, given that the CEECs are strong candidates to receive such payment, their integration will rekindle the debate on compensation schemes and increase pressure for their review. Net contributing members will likely argue on the basis of subsidiary that it is logical that nationally determined rates be financed nationally. Poorer countries will likely argue that richer countries will distort markets by proving more generous support to their farmers. The outcome of such debates will make a big difference to the impact of the CAP in the CEECs as well as the access of the CEECs to the CAP (Buckwell and Targermann, 1997).

[13] For example, for cereals, oilseeds and protein crops they are around 10 per cent, for sugar beet somewhere between 40-50 per cent, for dairy products in the order of 15-25 per cent, for beef in the region of 15-25 per cent, while for certain fruit and vegetables those price differences can be even up to 80 per cent (which is the case for tomatoes).

LONG -TERM OUTLOOK AND THE NEW CAP

According to the major international budgetary expenditure forecasting institutes, the long-term outlook for the main agricultural markets is favourable for exporting countries. Prospects for increased food consumption, mainly in developing countries, combined with the limited possibility of a proportionate growth in domestic production,[14] are expected to boost world trade and sustain world prices over the next decade.

Two key factors influence food demand: population growth and rising incomes. The world population is expected to increase by more than 85 million a year between 1995 and 2005. Moreover, growing urbanization will influence the pattern of food consumption. The second factor determining food demand is the favourable prospects for world incomes and economic growth, particularly in developing countries.

The wish to help European agriculture to take advantage of the expected positive world market developments, and to enable the prospect of enlargement of the EU to incorporate up to ten countries of Central and Eastern Europe (along with Cyprus) stimulated the Commission to come up with a blueprint for those aspects of the EU policy that are most affected. The blueprint was launched in 1997 as Agenda 2000. The main thrust of the document was that the budgetary implications of extending the regional and agricultural policies would be insupportable from current resources. Policy changes would be needed prior to enlargement to enable the EU to withstand the budgetary shock. Regarding the changes in agriculture policy, the Commission proposes in its Agenda 2000 the deepening and widening of the 1992 reform through further shifts from price support to direct payments and the development of a coherent rural policy to accompany this process. Lower prices will improve the competitiveness of EU agriculture on both domestic and external markets, benefit consumers and leave more room for price differentiation in favour of high quality speciality products. In addition, it will offer the EU increased flexibility in the next WTO Round negotiations. Environmental considerations[15] have become a major concern of the CAP which is adopting agricultural practices necessary to safeguard the environment and preserve the countryside.

At the Berlin Summit in March 1999, EU heads of government reached a global agreement on the reform of the CAP[16], which was less ambitious than the proposals of the Commission and the one that emerged form the March 11 Agricultural Council.

The reformed CAP represents a step towards supporting the broader rural economy rather than agricultural production and ensures that farmers are rewarded not only for what they produce but also for their general contribution to society. This means that the policy is targeted not just at agricultural producers but also at the wider rural population,

---

[14] These will be due to, firstly, the limited availability of land, because of urbanization and environmental constraints and, secondly, to a slowdown in the growth of yields.

[15] Since ratification of the Maastricht Treaty, there has been a legal obligation on the Union to take account of environmental protection requirements when drawing up and implementing Community policies. An obligation which was reinforced by the entry into force of the Treaty of Amsterdam on May 1, 1999.

[16] See e.g. E.C. *Agenda 2000* and **Agra Europe** (1999).

consumers and society as a whole. The political agreement resulted in the adoption of new regulations which came into force (with the exception of milk) from the year 2000 onwards. These concern the arable crops, beef, milk and wine sectors, the new rural development framework, the horizontal rules for direct schemes and the financing of the CAP. The amended regulations[17]for the olive oil and tobacco sectors have to be added to this list, even though they were not adopted in the context of the Agenda 2000 reform package. A transitional regime for olive oil was introduced in November 1998 with a view to undertaking wider-ranging reforms in 2001, and a fundamental reform of the tobacco sector has been implemented, aimed at encouraging production of higher quality tobacco varities in the EU and strengthening environmental protection.

EU leaders have agreed that the CAP budget[18] should remain "stable" over the next seven years. The budget target agreed for the CAP is Euro 40.5 billion a year on average plus 2 per cent inflation, plus Euro 14 billion of expenditure on rural development (Table 2). In effect, EU governments have handed greater fiscal control to the Commission in return for guarantees that spending will not exceed the Euro 40.5 billion target. In order to do so, the Commission will now be forced to watch its expenditure and make early savings in areas such as export refunds and intervention buying, if there is danger of exceeding its remit before the end of any given financial year. To evaluate this, the Council added a demand for a report in 2002 from the Commission "on the development of agricultural expenditure, accompanied, if necessary, by appropriate proposals".

---

[17] *Official Journal of the European Communities*, L 160, 26.06.99/ L 179, 14.07.99.

[18] Current budgetary discussions are of particular importance due to the implications the eastern enlargement will have on budgetary balances. During the period 2000-2006, the Commission is not expecting any changes in the relative budgetary position of the current member States. However, a recent discussion of budgetary imbalances in relation to the relative prosperity of member States has drawn attention to the possibility of granting budgetary corrections. In this respect, the performance of the compensation mechanism for the U.K. with the 1984 the Fontainebleau Agreement is questioned and the legitimacy of the decision is being reviewed. As the Commission reports, the British rebate distorts the whole system of contribution. The UK has 16.1 per cent of the EU GNP and pays 11.9 per cent of the budget. In contrast, Germany has 26 per cent of the EU GNP and pays 28.2 per cent of the budget costs, Greece 1.5 per cent and 1.65, respectively, France 17.2 per cent and 17.5 per cent. The only other country with a disproportional share of the budget is Italy with 14.2 per cent and 11.5 per cent (Josling and Babinard, 1999). Germany, as the biggest contributor, wishes to substantially reduce its net contribution to the EU budget form the present 22 billion DM a year. However, the Germans decided eventually to abandon "co-financing", a scheme under which national governments would have shared the costs of subsidizing the agriculture sector in their respective countries.

Table 2: Planned CAP expenditure 2000-06 (in million Euros, 1999 prices)

	2000	2001	2002	2003	2004	2005	2006
Heading1 (Agriculture)	**40920**	**42800**	**43900**	**43770**	**42760**	**41930**	**41660**
CAP expenditure (excluding rural development and accompanying measures)	36620	38480	39570	39430	38410	37570	37290
Rural development and accompanying measures	4300	4320	4330	4340	4350	4360	4370

Source: *Chairmanship's Conclusions,* 24 and 25 March 1999, Berlin.

In more detail, the reform comprises (E.C., 1999):

i.   *Lower institutional prices to encourage competitiveness*
     Reductions in market support prices ranging between 15 per cent for cereals and 20 per cent for beef will be introduced. A cut of 15 cent will apply to the milk sector from the year 2005/2006. The cuts will be introduced gradually with the objective of bringing Europe's farmers into closer touch with world market prices, thus helping improve the competitiveness of agricultural products on domestic and world markets with positive impacts on both internal demand and export levels. Equally important, the changes will contribute to the progressive integration of the new member States.

ii. *A fair standard of living for the farming community*
     The institutional price reductions will be partially offset by an increase in direct aid payments, thus contributing to the aim of providing farmers with a fair standard of living. The move away from price support towards direct income support for farmers means a further decoupling of aid from production.

iii. *Strengthening the EU's international trade position*
     Greater market orientation will help to reinforce the EU's position in the WTO negotiations.

iv. *Focus on quality*
     The reform takes full account of increased consumer concerns over food quality and safety, environmental protection and animal welfare in farming. Both in market support and in the new rural development policy compliance with minimum standards in the fields of environment, hygiene and animal welfare is a requirement.

v.   *An integration of environmental goals into the CAP*
     Member States have to introduce undertake environmental measures they consider appropriate. In fulfilling this obligation, member States would have three options at their disposal. In the first place, implementation of appropriate agri-envrironmental measures applied under rural development programmes may be sufficient. Secondly, member States may also make direct payments under the market organisations conditional on the observance of generally applicable environmental requirements. Thirdly, they may attach specific environmental

conditions to the granting of such payments. In the latter two cases, a proportionate reduction or cancellation of payments would be applied in cases of non-compliance.

vi. *A new rural development framework*

The new policy for rural development seeks to establish a coherent and sustainable framework for the future of Europe's rural areas. It will complement the reforms introduced into the market sectors by promoting a competitive, multi-functional agricultural sector in the context of a comprehensive, integrated strategy for rural development.

The guiding principles of the new policy are those of decentralisation of responsibilities thus strengthening subsidiarity and partnership- and flexibility of programming based on a "menu" of actions to be targeted and implemented according to member States' specific needs. As a coherent package of measures it has three main objectives:

- To create a stronger agricultural and forestry sector, the latter recognised for the first time as an integral part of the rural development policy;
- To improve the competitiveness of rural areas;
- To maintain the environment and preserve Europe's rural heritage

The environmental measures are the only compulsory element of the new generation of rural development programmes. The agri-environmental aid scheme will encourage farmers to introduce or continue to use farming practices compatible with environmental protection and natural resource conservation.

vii. *Decentralising management*

Direct payments to producers have been organised in a different way compared with 1992. Part of the direct payments for the beef and dairy sectors will take the form of a national financial envelope from the EAGGF budget which member States can distribute, thus allowing them to target specific national or regional priorities. Each member State will be able to allocate resources freely, subject to certain Community criteria designed to prevent distortions of competition.

CONCLUDING REMARKS

Given the historical background of the six original member countries, their agricultural structures and the fact that the EC-6 was a net importer of agricultural products, the CAP objectives, essentially about productivity gains in order to bolster the living standards of European farmers and to secure food supplies following the traumas of the 1940s and early 1950s, were neither surprising nor inappropriate. The same holds with respect to the choice of policy instruments, mainly internal price support. However, given the massive technical progress and structural shake-out which took place in the

European Community, the CAP soon was dominated by problems of chronic overproduction. It was not until mid-1992 that a significant reform took place under the intense pressure of the GATT Uruguay Round.

The reform resulted in a major shift from price support to forms of farm support not directly linked to production. After 1992, there have been considerable market improvements with significantly lower public stocks in most of the reformed sectors (except in the case of beef, which is due to extraordinary events rather than market policy). Moreover, farm incomes have markedly improved over the period.

However, the progress achieved was not sufficient to meet the challenges facing the EU in the light of the WTO negotiations (which would push EU agriculture to a freer trade regime) on the one hand and the EU's eastern enlargement on the other hand. Taking into consideration that the CEECs farm prices are 40 to 80 per cent those of the EU's, the adoption of the *acquis communautaire* would increase the surplus of principal agricultural products in the majority of the candidate countries. Thus, it would place great pressure on the finely balance arrangements of the WTO Agreement. The Commission, having reviewed these prospects and the expected positive world market developments, concluded that the best option was to continue the 1992 approach through further shifts from price support to direct payments and the development of a more integrated rural policy to accompany this process. However, the agreement reached at the recent Berlin Summit is less ambitious than the Commission's proposals included in Agenda 2000. As a result, a delay is expected in the EU's eastward enlargement. The EU's negotiating position in future WTO negotiations will be formulated along the lines of the Berlin Agreement, which falls far short of the US objectives regarding the liberalization of international trade in agricultural commodities. More specifically, the approach of the EU to the next round negotiations can be summarised as follows. On the question of access to the markets, the EU will declare itself against any drastic reduction in tariffs. On export subsidies, it will maintain that these are essential to the clearing of markets, at least for the next few years, while on other questions the EU has already expressed its intention to re-negotiate the Sanitary and Phytosanitary Standards Agreement to take into account situations where consumer concerns are being underpayed by market considerations. Last, since the CAP reform was decided before the next round of WTO negotiations, the changes adopted will reflect clearly the international constraints on the EU and will strengthen the EU negotiating position in the WTO round.

After the introduction of the compensatory payments in 1992, a considerable wave of dissent has been rising within the EU on the issue of subsidiarity and on the idea that some elements of the CAP should be financed by national governments. The budget issue is especially controversial due to the differences in the contributions by individual member States and to the impact of CAP on EU expenditure as a whole. Nevertheless, over the next seven years it will be the first time in the EU's history that spending on agriculture will not have shown constant growth in real terms.

Proposals for the further "greening" of the CAP included in Agenda 2000 have been adopted in the Berlin Agreement. These comprise support and remuneration to farmers for services to the environment as well as for their contribution to the maintenance of the rural heritage within the EU and have encouraged the transformation of the CAP from an essentially agricultural policy to one of environmental and rural development.

REFERENCES

1. Agra Europe (1999):"Berlin Summit Tears CAP Reforms Deal Apart", March 26, No 1842: 1-7.

2. Baltas, N. C. (1997): "The Restructed CAP and the Periphery of the EU", *Food Policy*, 22(4):329-343.

3. Baltas, N.C. (1998): "Greek Agriculture under the CAP: The Experience of the First Fifteen Years". Published in: C. Paraskevopoulos (Ed), *European Union at the Crossroads: A Critical Analysis of Monetary Union and Enlargement*, U.K. Edward Elgar Publishing Limited, Aldershot, Chapter 7, pp.134-149.

4. Brittan, Sir Leon (1999): "The Next WTO Negotiations on Agriculture, A European View", Paper presented to the 53rd Oxford Farming Conference, 5 January.

5. Buckwell, A. and Targermann, S.(1997): "The CAP and Central and Eastern Europe". Published in C. Ritson and D.R. Harvey (Eds), *The Common Agricultural Policy* (2nd Edition) CAB International, Oxford, U.K.

6. Coleman, W.D. and Tangermann, S. (1999): "The 1992 CAP Reform, the Uruguay Round and the Commission: Conceptualizing Linked Policy Games", *Journal of Common Market Studies*, 37(3): 385-405.

7. Delorme, H., and Clerc, D. (1994): *Un nouveau Gatt? Les enchanges Mondiales apres l'Uruguay Round*, Editions Complexe, Paris.

8. E.C. (1999): *CAP Reform: A Policy for the Future*, Directorate General of Agriculture, Brussels.

9. E.C. (1998): Prospects for Agricultural Markets, 1998-2000, Brussels.

10. E. C.(1997): *Agenda 2000: For a Stronger and Wider Union*, Bulletin of the European Union, supplement 5/97, Brussels.

11. E. C. (1997) : "The CAP and Enlargement", *European Economy*, No 2.

12. E.C. (1995): *The Agricultural Situation in the European Union*, 1994 Report, Brussels, Luxemburg.

13. Harvey, D (1997): "The GATT, the WTO and the CAP". Published in C. Ritson and D.R. Harvey (Eds), *The Common Agricultural Policy* (2nd Ed.), CAB International, Oxford, U.K.

14. Josling, T. and Babinard, J. (1999): "The Future of the CAP and Prospects for Change: The Policy Environment for Agri-Food Competitiveness". Published in: ISMEA, *The European Agro-Food System and the Challenges of Global Competition*, Roma, Italy.

15. Josling, T. (1994): "The Reformed CAP and the Industrial World", *European Review of Agricultural Economics*, 21:513-527.

16. Jovanovic, M.N. (2000): "Eastern Enlargement of the European Union: Sour Grapes or Sweet Lemon?", Paper presented at the European Summer School, Spetsae Island (Greece), July 3-8, 2000.

17. Mergos, G. (1998) "Agricultural Issues in Integration of CEECs in the EU". Published in N. Baltas, et.al. *Economic Interdependence and Cooperation in Europe*, Springer-Verlag, Heidelberg.

18. O.E.C.D. (1995): "The Uruguay Round Agreement: A Preliminary Evaluation of the Impacts of the Agreement on Agriculture in the OECD Countries", Paris.

19. Swinbank, A. (1993): "CAP Reform, 1993", *Journal of Common Market Studies,*31: 359-372.

20. Swinbank, A. and Ritson, C. (1995): "The Impact of the GATT Agreement on EU Fruits and Vegetables Policy", *Food Policy,* 20(4): 339-357.

Chapter 8

OPEN WINDOWS OF EUROPE

Caroline A. Rodenburg, Barry Ubbels and Peter Nijkamp
Department of spatial economics
Vrije Universiteit Amsterdam
De Boelelaan 1105, 1081 HV Amsterdam The Netherlands

ABSTRACT

The future of the transport sector is fraught with uncertainties, as the system is influenced by many factors. The aim of this paper is to offer insight into the future of this sector, seen from a European perspective, by applying a scenario approach and designing four possible paths of development. These future developments are presented here by a sketch of four contrasting European images based on the results of earlier research. The outcome for the transport sector, expressed in volumes for both passenger and freight, are qualitatively described and based on expected developments of several relevant indicators. Subsequently, the results are presented in terms of CO_2 emissions, with major focus on the EU. With these results in mind, it is interesting to confront the EU's objectives and current policies. Creating sustainable mobility appeared to be a key element in EU transport policy. Nevertheless, the achievement of sustainable mobility based on the results presented in this paper may seem problematic and will face several hurdles. But policy changes and (unexpected) technology developments may offer new possibilities to achieve a steadier development of the transport sector.

INTRODUCTION

An efficient transport system is a crucial precondition for economic development and an asset for local, regional and international mobility. The mobility of passengers and free transport of goods is considered an important element for a modern society. Transport has become a major economic sector with the integration of the world market, economic growth and higher levels of income. This can be illustrated, for example, by the contribution of the transport sector to the GDP. This figure is estimated at around 7 percent for Europe, and 8 percent in The Netherlands (Geerlings, 1997). This gives an indication of the importance of transport. The significance of this sector may even exceed these proportions, as no economic activity can flourish without transportation. It is clear that mobility has become a prerequisite for the proper functioning of modern societies.

The transport sector is subject to drastic changes and various trends. In the nearby future, changes in modal split and growth in mobility will have a direct impact on it. The role of transport policies will be another influencing factor. The increasing attention to market incentives and the move towards harmonization (a recent policy trend of the European Union) are aspects that may have a significant impact on this development. So the future of the transport sector is fraught with uncertainties, as the system could be influenced by many factors which could develop in various ways.

The aim of this paper is to gain insight into the future developments in the transportation sector up until 2020, seen from a European perspective. This is achieved by designing four paths of development for the transportation sector. We start out with four globalization scenarios, constructed in an earlier phase of our research[1]. These globalization developments will form the input for the transport scenarios, which are elaborated on a European scale. The mentioned globalization scenarios were first qualitatively described and then quantified with the help of the Worldscan model of the CPB (see CPB, 1999). The results of the assessment are used as a guiding tool. The consequences of the scenarios will be expressed in clear numbers of transported volumes in 2020 (in ton-kilometers for freight and passenger-kilometers for passenger transport). This enables us to obtain more insight into the size of transport flows in order to estimate future transport emissions. This is an extremely important challenge, as all European countries have committed themselves to the Kyoto agreement in order to drastically cut CO_2 emissions. Thus, the achievement of sustainable transport is a major policy objective, and an exploration of alternative futures is crucial.

This paper is organized as follows. The next section will deal with general remarks concerning scenarios in the decision-making process. Section 3 gives a theoretical overview of the construction of scenarios and will describe certain types of scenarios as well as the possibilities in scale and time. The fourth section provides an overview of the European setting and the expected developments on a European scale, before describing consequences for future developments in European transport, based on four qualitative European scenarios. The subsequent section will show the consequences of the European scenarios in relation to the European sustainability policy. Conclusions are drawn in Section 6.

---

[1] Globalization, International Transport and the Global Environment (GITAGE), writing transport scenarios is one of the tasks of this project funded by NWO, see also van Veen-Groot et al., 1998.

SCENARIOS IN DECISION-MAKING

Scenarios are descriptions of future developmenikDIUhWned on explicit assumptions that could have an important role in the decision-making process. Decision-making relies heavily on information that can be provided by scenarios. In general, existing information is not endQoY2BuC often does not fulfil the needs of decision-makers, neither in a quantitative nor a qualitative sense (Rienstra, 1998). This causes uncertainty about the likelihood of future developments.

The transport system is such an open system that uncertainty always exists. The system cannot be fully controlled but is subject to many factors. Therefore it is difficult to predict which developments in these systems are likely to occur in the future. This uncertainty can be reduced in various ways. For example, decision-makers have decision-support tools at their disposal. One of these tools are scenarios, which have the following functions (see e.g. Steenbergen, 1983):

- The signaling function: scenarios provide greater insight into uncertain situations.
- The communications and learning function: scenarios stimulate thoughts about alternative futures and provide decision-makers with options.
- The legitimization function: scenarios mobilize people and start processes of change when they show the impact if nothing is done, or when the future situation in the scenario seems beneficial.
- The exploring and explaining function: scenarios show how solutions for specific problems may become reality, given certain policy priorities.
- The demonstration function: scenarios show the consequences of specific decisions.

Scenarios enable us to reduce complexity and facilitate discussions about future events by arranging and classifying information and preventing information overload (Rienstra, 1998). Scenarios may help in gaining insight into the consequences of strategies and help to compare the consequences of the choice for a certain strategy. Scenarios in this way can provide us with new insights into possible paths and policies and their impacts on the future.

It should be noted that scenarios could be constructed in various ways, using different methods, and leading to different contents. They may be intuitive or a literary product, idealistic or based on qualitative assessment. Scenarios are structured brainstorming methods created to widen the perceptions of policy makers and researchers regarding future possibilities and policy options.

Transport has a strategic role in most economies and is an important tool for politicians and governments in stimulating economic growth. Governments use transport to gain or increase competitive advantage on other countries. Nevertheless, transport has a lot of negative consequences such as the external impact on the environment. Since there are often conflicting interests in the field of (future) transport, scenarios can provide the tool for coming to solid future expectations/descriptions.

TRANSPORT SCENARIOS

We have described the importance of scenarios in decision making. The scenarios describe future expectations in the field of transport, divided into expectations for freight and passenger transport. Transport refers to the movement of people, information and goods and has become one of the key activities in modern society. Transport scenarios are seen here as pictures of the future within the specified framework of the movement of goods and persons. The scenarios can be described on the basis of different characteristics of transport (e.g. volume, spatial organization, modal split, and transport technology, distance and emission factors). The construction of these scenarios will give insight into the future developments of the transportation sector. It is important to bear in mind that the foreseen developments in transport are directly derived from global developments as described in four globalization scenarios (Van Veen-Groot, et al., 1999). From this follows the distinction between two regions (OECD vs. non-OECD on a world scale), which also forced us to make a division on a European level (EU versus non-EU, see below).

This structure is followed through in the next sections, which describe the various transport scenarios. In order to describe changes in transport volume properly (used here as a characteristic to express changes in transport) four aspects of transport are described. Spatial organization, distance, technological development and modal split will all have a certain impact on transported volumes and can be seen as indicators. Each scenario will close with an overview (combined for spatial organization and distance, and excluding modal split) of (expected) impact on the various aspects on the modalities in Europe (EU (members of the European Union (+ Iceland, Norway and Switzerland) vs. non-EU) in table-form. These tables are filled with indicators (+, 0, -) expressing the expected impact on modalities of the various developments described in the scenarios. The situation as it was in 1995 was taken as a starting point: this is the reference situation. A plus in transport volume only means that it is expected that the volume of goods or persons transported by a certain mode will grow in comparison to the reference situation. As a consequence, double plus means that a stronger positive development is expected. It is important to keep in mind, however, that the plusses do not necessarily have the same meaning within the diverse aspects and scenarios, nor within a scenario. A plus for technology impact on transport volume is not comparable with a plus for distance/spatial organization). They can only be regarded as indicators of a positive, a neutral or a negative development (in case of a minus). In the description here, a zero does not mean that the situation will not change during the period of time. It only indicates that compared to the reference situation, no significant change is to be expected.

Scenario 1: Growth

In this scenario, there are high economic growth rates in the EU as well as in non-EU countries. Production and consumption will take place on a European scale, which produces a rise in transportation flows within Europe, as a result of the increasing demand of users for transport services. The non-EU countries should open up to allow foreign goods and foreign investment. By opening up, the dissemination of technologies from Western Europe will be accelerated in non-EU countries. Eastern Europe benefits from the overflow from Western Europe to come to economic prosperity. The EU and non-EU countries will grow towards each other and closer economic integration between rich and poor countries will result. Finally, the distinction between non-EU and EU will become weaker and expansion of the EU will become realistic.

Because of the 'Europeanization' of production and consumption, it is likely that the average distance covered by the diverse transport modes will increase. The economic growth in non-EU countries will lead to a convergence of consumer preferences towards the EU (CPB, 1999). This increase in transport applies not only to passenger transport, but also to freight transport.

The progress of new transportation technologies in combination with high economic growth rates will cause an increase in mobility and transport throughout Europe. The national governments want to stimulate economic growth. Transport is assumed to be necessary to accomplish this, so public infrastructure for the diverse transport modes will have to be constructed. This scenario predicts a considerable growth in international air and high-speed rail transport. Especially the introduction and expansion of high-speed rail will have its impact and will cause a shift between the diverse transport modes. The future of road transport is somewhat unsure, however. There are improvements to be expected concerning fuel and engine technologies, but these will not have a significant impact on the use of the car as a means of transport. This will just reduce negative impacts on the environment in a modest way. There will also be a trend towards intermodal transport. Because of the growing volume of transport flows, other/new transportation systems will be used to transport larger quantities of goods and to cover the new routes, as well as reach new destinations. The European mainports, which will support this trend, will have the latest transport technology at their disposal.

As a result of the prosperous economic situation in Europe, the more expensive (but faster) transport modes will become more generally used. For passenger transport, this means that air and high-speed rail transport will be more widely used, and will form a substitute for road transportation. The main part of this shift in modality will take place in Western Europe, where the means to develop and to enlarge such a system are more easily available than in Eastern Europe. For freight transportation, an increase in performance is to be expected, since current performance is rather low, and with the progress in transport technology, freight transport by rail will benefit from this development.

In response to the liberalization of goods markets and lower transport costs (CPB, 1999), international specialization becomes more pronounced This, together with the trend towards 'Europeanization', will lead to increased flows in freight transportation. In passenger transport, growth also is foreseen. Due to the rise in income, people will make more trips for consumption reasons, including leisure and shopping. The growth in consumption as well as the growth in production will lead to increased transport volume. More people have to travel to work, education and training. The former mentioned technology might reduce this trend, but to a lesser extent.

Trans European Networks (TEN's) will play an important role in this scenario. The development of the TEN's will influence the spatial organization in Europe. As a result of these networks, transport flows will concentrate on specific infrastructures. Such networks will not only occur in road transport but will be developed for rail transportation as well. As a consequence, transfer points in these networks will develop into large mainports. High-speed networks for rail transport will especially be implemented in the EU countries where they have the latest transport technology at their disposal. The nodes in the TEN's will become the focal points of economic growth, production and population.

Table 1: Scenario 1: Growth

		Spatial organization/ Distance		Transport technology		Volume	
		EU	Non-EU	EU	Non-EU	EU	Non-EU
Freight transport	Air	+	+	+	+	+	+
	Road	+	++	+	++	++	++
	Rail	++	+	+	++	+	++
	Seaborne shipping	+	+	+	+	++	+
	Inland shipping	+	+	+	+	+	+
Pass. transp.	Air	+	+	+	+	+	++
	Road	+	++	+	++	+	++
	Rail	++	++	++	++	++	++

Scenario 2: Core-growth

This scenario assumes that governments in Eastern European countries are not able to pursue market oriented and outward oriented policies. The political situation in most of these countries is unstable and leads to an introspective attitude. This is in contrast to the development of the EU where high economic progress exists. The prosperous economic situation in the EU countries is combined with high technological progress and intensive trade with the rest of the world. The expectation that the EU will be enlarged with other countries is unlikely.

In order to control this economic growth and to retain its competitive position in the world, a strong European Union is to be expected. Economic efficiency in the transport sector will be enhanced and economic development stimulated. The EU will succeed in reducing the missing links; for example, the Trans-European networks will be completed. Apart from efficiency goals, new infrastructure links are also being built to ensure cohesion in the EU space (equity). As the Eastern European countries are inward oriented and unwilling to participate they will not be enclosed in these networks. Policies will aim to equalize economic activities, welfare and population over the EU, which will largely be achieved by expanding EU cohesion and regional development funds. Trade and transport will be concentrated within the EU countries.

Road networks will not be the first priority; as a result of the sustainability objective, harbors are far more important. Airports will expand in the booming regions, because air transport will be far more efficiently organized (especially within the EU). They will mainly facilitate intercontinental transport. Consequently, harbors and mainports will become crucial. They will act as intercontinental, national and regional points of transhipment where different transport modes meet up. Locations where air and rail meet are also becoming significant. Economic activities will take place in and around these major locations and new techniques will be used to support the development of these transfer points. The development of networks in Eastern Europe lags behind and there is no real concentration of spatial activities. There is a lack of network infrastructure and mainports remain underdeveloped, mainly due to the inward orientation of government policies.

The distances over which goods and passengers have to be transported will increase within the EU countries. The kilometers covered by air transport will show the fastest growth in freight transport, followed by the kilometers covered by rail transportation of passengers. The distance covered by road transport is growing too, but to a lesser degree because of the technological development of other logistics in commuter transport. Physical distance will become less important because of improved telecommunication technologies. In Eastern European countries, however, road transport will flourish as a result of the lack of other innovative transportation.

The technological progress is one of the driving factors behind the economic growth in EU countries. New (transportation) technologies will be developed and applied fairly soon. Especially air and rail technologies will improve in these sectors and become more important within the EU. New (ICT) techniques will facilitate the efficient operation of high-speed rail networks. Air transportation, in turn, will improve in efficiency because of new radar systems and improved communications. Technical developments will also take place in the motor car system but to a lesser degree, and will solely relate to a lower consumption of fuel. Electric cars will improve, but a major breakthrough is not anticipated.

Eastern European countries will increasingly rely on already existing techniques. Slowly certain new techniques will be imported from other countries but on a small scale. The techniques will be implemented first in those sectors where innovation is strong in European Union countries (e.g. air and rail).

It is obvious that as a result of economic growth, the more expensive (but faster) travel/transportation modes will become serious options for a wider public. For passenger transport, this means that intercontinental air transport and high-speed rail transport will become more popular compared to road transport. Freight will be organized more traditionally in the EU; road networks will remain dominant, although inland waterways will take over a considerable share. In terms of long distance freight transport, sea shipping and air transport will become dominant, supported by the development of networks and mainports.

Eastern Europe, on the other hand, has no flourishing trade. Governments do not stimulate investment in infrastructure. As a result these non-EU countries will rely on already available transportation modes and related techniques. Road transport is still the dominant mode of passenger and freight transport in developing countries.

The demand for transport is paramount in the economic progress of EU countries. It is obvious that this leads to increased flows in freight and passenger transportation. Developments in the general economic situation, spatial organization, technology and modal split will lead to changes in volume. Eastern European countries will still be mainly dependent on road transport as no important new developments are expected. As a result, this will have an impact on transport volumes.

Table 2: Scenario 2: Core-Growth

		Spatial organization/ Distance		Transport technology		Volume	
		EU	Non-EU	EU	Non-EU	EU	Non-EU
Freight transport	Air	++	0	++	+	++	+
	Road	+	+	+	0	+	+
	Rail	+	0	++	+	+	0
	Seaborne shipping	++	+	++	+	++	+
	Inland shipping	+	0	+	0	++	0
Pass. transp.	Air	+	0	++	+	+	0
	Road	+	+	+	0	++	+
	Rail	++	0	++	0	++	0

Scenario 3: Peripheral growth

In the first two scenarios, a rosy picture of the EU countries was described. They benefited from external factors such as the economic growth in non-EU countries, or they themselves generated high economic growth rates. In this scenario, however, the emphasis will be on Eastern Europe (the non-EU countries). The European Union did not manage to generate important technology breakthroughs, which enabled Eastern Europe to make up on arrears on the basis of existing conventional technologies. This means that mainly the energy-intensive technologies from the EU countries will be copied, due to the lack of energy-extensive innovations in non-EU countries. As a result, the demand for energy will rise substantially, resulting in an increase of emissions (van Veen-Groot, 1999).

The EU countries will face a drop in economic growth, caused by a limited availability of resources and a slow-down in the progress of technological development (van Veen-Groot, 1999). Economic crises in the EU will strengthen protectionist sentiments and slow down international trade. The Eastern European trade blocks will make sure that the main point of trade and transport will shift from the EU towards Eastern Europe. As the main transport flows are found in these regions, this will result in an increase in emissions. Nevertheless, the non-EU countries will start to develop networks that connect Eastern European countries, enabling them to meet the growing demand for goods and transport.

The average distance covered by the diverse transport modes will increase in Eastern Europe, thanks to the prosperous economy and growing trade (not only regional, but also international). In Western Europe, the growth will be lower, due to the unstable economic situation. As a result of the strong economic growth in Eastern Europe, the demand for goods and the demand for passenger transportation will rise.

New technologies will not be invented because of the restrained economic situation in the EU. Non-EU countries will copy existing innovations and technologies from the EU before they introduce their own. This means that new transportation technologies are not to be expected. Among the latest technologies from Western Europe, the biggest improvements are to be found in road transportation. The attention of the non-EU countries will mainly be on bigger and more luxurious road vehicles, which will have a negative influence on the environment. Improvements in air transportation are also to be expected, mainly because of the updating of current fleets to further ensure the safety of passengers. In rail transportation, there will be a change from fuel trains to electric trains.

Some major changes in modal split are to be foreseen. In Eastern Europe, the more expensive and faster travel modes will become available to a wider public. This means that a modal shift will take place from road passenger transport to rail, and especially air transport. Major investments are being made in rail infrastructure, so that trains can use double instead of single tracks. This will produce an increase in the number of passengers, since travelling by train is becoming far more convenient and efficient. Nevertheless, the main growth is to be expected in road transport, which is still the transport mode with the most capacity and the lowest costs. It is also the mode that requires the least effort in expanding, and meets the growing demand for the transportation of goods and passengers. Western European countries will show a medium growth in air and shipping because of the strong prevailing trend towards these transport systems, and the lower tendency towards road transport.

Due to the economic situation in Eastern Europe, the demand for goods will rise. Consumers in non-EU countries will change their consumption patterns in line with that of EU countries. This means that more goods will have to be transported, most likely over larger distances and the volume of transported goods will rise. In Eastern Europe, passenger transport is likely to increase as well. In Western Europe, the volume of transport flows will stay more or less equal, although some growth in air and sea transport is expected. Due to the unstable economic situation, a substantial growth in demand for goods and passenger transportation is not foreseen.

Table 3: Scenario 3: Peripheral Growth

		Spatial organization/ Distance		Transport technology		Volume	
		EU	Non-EU	EU	Non-EU	EU	Non-EU
Freight transport	Air	0	++	0	++	+	++
	Road	+	++	+	++	0	++
	Rail	0	+	0	++	0	+
	Seaborne shipping	+	+	+	+	+	+
	Inland shipping	+	+	+	+	0	+
Pass. transp.	Air	0	++	0	++	+	++
	Road	+	++	+	++	0	+
	Rail	0	+	0	++	0	++

Scenario 4: Sustainable growth

The previous scenarios all took the level of economic growth as a starting point, and the environment was a minor aspect. In contrast, this scenario concentrates on the environment. Environmental quality within Europe is regarded as the driving force. Economic growth is not neglected but is only important within the constraints of wellbeing and (environmental) quality of life. Society as a whole is aware of the need to create and enhance a sustainable development.

Production and consumption will be more local but continue to take place in the EU more than in non-EU countries. While local transport between regions will predominate, development of the European-wide road networks will stagnate. Trains will take over long distance travel. Points of transfer will increase as multimodal and collective transport grows. Especially rail/sea and air/sea movement will grow. Seen from this perspective, harbors and mainports will largely affect the efficiency of multimodal transport and are vital in this development.

Overall, on both sides of Europe, one can see that transport distances will remain stable and transport flows will be bundled. Air transport may retain its share, as it is mainly used for international travel and long distances. Within Europe, passenger rail transport will take over distances that were formerly covered by air transportation. For the passage of freight, the same holds true for inland and sea shipping. Road transport will also lose part of its share (more in passenger than in freight transport) because private transport will become more expensive.

This scenario foresees an important role for technological development in realizing a more sustainable society. All over Europe new transport technologies will be vital for a sustainable economic development. Growing environmental awareness will accelerate the acceptation of new, less polluting, applications. Large-scale investments in infrastructure will be made, and new techniques will be implemented and mostly directed towards improvement of the energy efficiency of the various types of transport vehicles. The implementation of technological applications will be substantial: new IT possibilities, electric cars and new forms of public transport will become common. The EU will export its technology to Eastern European countries.

Innovations affecting road transport will be higher in Eastern Europe than in the EU as the latter already own cleaner cars and trucks. In the EU more attention will be paid to energy efficient techniques and the application of new telematics (e.g. dynamic route information) to increase capacity of existing infrastructure. The aviation sector will also improve. New airplanes will be introduced which will be fuelled with liquid hydrogen. Innovations in logistics will improve multimodal transport and give a push to the transportation of freight by rail and water. Railway and urban public transport will expand because of improved technological developments and increasing capacity of existing infrastructures. Environmental awareness will also be expressed by growth in collective transport modes in both EU and non-EU countries. Individual transport will lose market share and become less important.

Although improvements are expected from the technology push in most polluting modes, it is still foreseen that rail, other public transport and shipment will claim a larger share in future. The use of public transport (improvements in service and infrastructure) will grow in densely populated areas and bigger cities. Also ICT will be implemented as a substitute for physical transport. The growth of air passenger transport will be limited because of the construction of subsidized HST tracks all over Europe. In order to save the environment and to overcome resistance from society, the HST is mainly using upgraded tracks. As for freight transport in Europe, seaborne shipping will become more important as multimodal transport is carried out more efficiently and it is regarded as environmentally friendly. Inland shipping will grow as a result of an improved competitive position with regard to road transport.

The foregoing aspects will have an impact on the volume of transport flows. In this environmental scenario, transportation will change as it is generally seen as a significant contributor to the environmental problems in our current society. It is anticipated that technology will help in reducing these negative effects (which affect all modes) and create a shift towards cleaner ones. In the transportation of freight, it is expected that the aviation and the rail sectors will grow. This development is facilitated by the change in spatial organization (mainports) and new technologies aimed at improved logistics. Rail and public transport (collective modes) will largely substitute passenger transport. Again it will draw passengers from road transport, as individual transport is not attractive.

Table 4: Scenario 4: Sustainable Growth

		Spatial organization/ Distance		Transport technology		Volume	
		EU	Non-EU	EU	Non-EU	EU	Non-EU
Freight transport	Air	+	+	+	+	+	+
	Road	0	+	+	++	0	0
	Rail	+	+	+	+	+	+
	Seaborne shipping	+	+	++	+	++	+
	Inland shipping	+	+	++	++	++	++
Pass. transp.	Air	+	+	+	+	0	+
	Road	-	0	+	++	0	0
	Rail	+	+	++	++	++	+

Overview

The description of the various scenarios in the previous sections ended with an overview of expected changes in transported volumes based on developments in transport technology, modal split and spatial organization/distance. The main outcomes are presented in Table 5, which provides a comparison of the four different European transportation scenarios.

These developments will have consequences for the transported volumes in terms of ton-kilometers and passenger-kilometers. Based on a tentative weighting of the various developments (expressed in terms of plusses, minuses or no changes) relative changes in volumes are expressed (see Table 6 for a comparison of the four scenarios).

From this table it becomes clear that there are quite some differences between the developments in transport volumes in the different scenarios on a European level. In scenario 1, for example, all distinguished transport modes for both passenger and freight in the EU will grow in terms of transported volumes. It might be clear that sustainable growth expects some particular modes to grow whereas road transport is likely not to show any difference compared with 1995. Now that these changes are clear and insight into some future developments has been clarified, it is interesting to estimate what the consequences are in terms of emissions (CO_2). This will be done in the next sections with the focus on the EU.

Table 5: Summarization of scenarios

	Growth	Core-growth	Peripheral growth	Sustainable growth
Spatial organization	• *Europeani-zation of production and consumption* • *Concentration on mainports* • *Development of Trans European Networks*	• *Importance of networks, harbors and mainports in EU* • *Concentration of trade and transport within EU*	• *Concentration of trade and transport within non-EU*	• *Localized production and consumptio n* • *Importance of harbors*
Distance	• *Increase of average distance*	• *Major increase of average distance within EU* • *Minor increase of average distance within non-EU*	• *Major increase of average distance within non-EU* • *Minor increase of average distance within EU*	• *Stabilizatio n of average distance within Europe*
Transport technology	• *High progress of new transportation technologies* • *Terminal facilities will be improved* • *Innovations on management level: ICT facilities*	• *High progress of new transportation technologies, especially in air and rail for EU* • *Terminal facilities will be improved in EU* • *ICT will be booming*	• *Improvement in technology mainly in non-EU* • *Increase of the use of ICT in non-EU*	• *Increase of efficiency of traditional modes* • *More improveme nts than other scenarios*
Modal split	• *Growth of international air and high-speed rail transport* • *Increase of intermodal transport*	• *Increase of air transport* • *Rail mainly important within EU (high-speed)* • *Overall importance of road transport (but restrained; due to fair and efficient pricing)* • *Sea transport important for freight*	• *Fast growth of road, air and rail in non-EU* • *Medium growth of air and shipping in EU*	• *ICT is a substitute of physical transport* • *Use of seaborne shipping important* • *Less leisure transport (due to high prices)*

Table 6: Changes in European Volume

		Growth		Core-growth		Peripheral growth		Sustainable growth	
		EU	non-EU	EU	non-EU	EU	non-EU	EU	non-EU
Freight transport	Air	+	+	++	+	+	++	+	+
	Road	++	++	+	+	0	++	0	0
	Rail	+	++	+	0	0	+	+	+
	Seaborne shipping	++	+	++	+	+	+	++	+
	Inland shipping	+	+	++	0	0	+	++	++
Pass. transp.	Air	+	++	+	0	+	++	0	+
	Road	+	++	+	+	0	+	0	0
	Rail	++	++	++	0	0	++	++	+

EMISSIONS FOR THE EUROPEAN UNION

The previous section described the various scenarios in a detailed way, which resulted in identified changes in transported volumes with regard to the reference situation (1995). The main thought behind this presentation in volumes was related to the next phase: calculating the emissions. These transported volumes (in terms of ton-kilometers (concerning freight transport) and passenger-kilometers (concerning passenger transport) are a prerequisite to calculate the consequences in terms of emissions (the focus is here on CO_2 emissions). So quantitative data had to be obtained concerning transported volumes in 2020. This information, together with assumptions about the development of energy efficiency of the various modes, enables us to derive the expected CO_2 emissions of road transport for 2020 in the EU (including Norway, Iceland and Switzerland). In this section we will shortly discuss the method we used to obtain these emission figures. For more detailed information on the calculation of quantitative volumes, we refer to Nijkamp et al. (2000) and for the final emissions, we refer to Olsthoorn (2000).

In an earlier section it was elucidated that the transport scenarios are derived from globalization scenarios. These global images were quantified by using the Worldscan model (see CPB, 1999). This resulted in growth rates between 1995 and 2020 for certain aspects such as GDP and real producer prices. These outcomes (especially trade and economic growth) enabled us to compose growth rates for transport in Europe for both passenger and freight transport. Taking the transported volumes in 1995 as a starting point, we can calculate the total transport volume in 2020. Further, the growth in this period is allocated over the various modes, distinguishing between passenger transport and freight transport (because of different unities). In allocating this growth the various changes in volumes, as presented in Table 6, are taken into account. This resulted in new volumes for each mode in each scenario. These volumes formed the input for the calculation of emissions. The CO_2 emissions were calculated based on several (energy efficiency) assumptions (Olsthoorn, 2000).

Figure 1 gives an overview of the CO_2 emissions caused by the various modes for the reference year and the four scenarios. From this figure it becomes clear that road transport has the biggest share in the total emissions. Scenario 1 shows a relatively large growth in emissions compared to scenario 3 and 4. Scenario 4 does not differ that much from the situation in 1995, so even in an EU country with a strong environmental awareness, it is not likely that emissions will decrease in the next 20 years. It should be kept in mind though that the scenarios do not contain concrete transport policies. Various policy measures could steer the development in a more desired direction, which would affect the outcomes presented here. It might be clear that the results of scenario 1 (Growth) and 2 (Core growth) are incompatible with a sustainable development. It is therefor interesting to see what current EU transport policy encloses and what the expected impact on emissions is of these measures in relation to the objectives and the scenarios. The next section will deal with these aspects.

Figure 1: CO_2 emissions in the European Union (Gtonne)

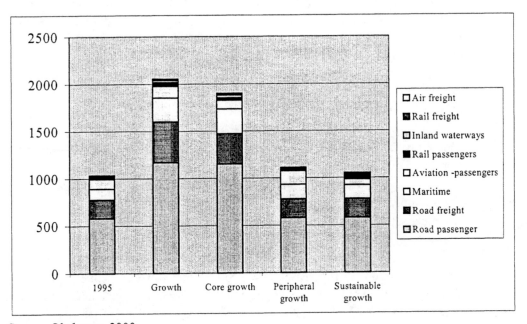

Source: Olsthoorn. 2000

EUROPEAN TRANSPORT POLICY

Currently the European transport policy is known as the Common Transport Policy (CTP). EU transport policy was elaborated by the Commission in the 1992 white paper, entitled "The future development of the CTP" (CEC, 1992). This document suggested that future initiatives should focus on certain components, such as safety and environmental protection. The aim should be to move away from a single market based approach to a more comprehensive policy, designed to ensure the proper functioning of the transport systems. After this the strategy was further refined in 1995 when the Commission published its follow-up paper for a CTP action program. It stated that efficient, accessible and competitive transport systems are vital to the society and the economy of the Union. An update of this program has recently been published and aims at Sustainable Mobility (CEC, 1998). The completion of the single market, safety issues, environmental protection, fair and efficient pricing and economic and social cohesion will be the main priorities in the coming years until 2004. Sustainable mobility is the keyword in current policy within the EU. This means encouraging the development of efficient and environmentally friendly transport systems that are safe and socially acceptable. Looking to the future, the efficiency of transport systems remains a fundamental objective for the competitiveness of Europe and for growth and employment. This object must go hand in hand with the need to make transport more sustainable. In other words, the CTP must offer a framework for sustainable mobility. The Commission includes a list of policy initiatives to be taken. Some important initiatives in the context of emissions will be highlighted briefly:

- Environment: the Commission will strengthen its environmental assessment of policy initiatives with important environmental effects, especially in the light of CO_2 emissions and climatic change.
- Trans European Networks: encouragement to speed up the implementation of the priority projects defined at the Essen Summit.
- Fair and efficient pricing in transport: the Commission will take the necessary steps to apply progressively the principle of charging for marginal social costs. This means that transport users also have to pay for external costs such as congestion and noise.

This short description gives a good indication of the aim and scope of transport policy in Europe. It may be clear that the aim is to crs economore sustainable transport system. Although discussion is possible on the explanation of sustainability in clear targets (weak and strong sustainability), it is imperative that the level of transport pollution should be curbed as much as possible. The level of CO_2 emissions, explicitly mentioned in the initiativ be invene of the key targets. From this it may be clear that the objective of the CTP is that the CO_2 emissions from transport will not grow and a decrease in emissions is even more desirable. In addition, a decrease is demanded by the Kyoto protocol (an 8% decrease of CO_2 emissions in 2010). If we look at the proposed outcomes of the various scenarios it is apparent that a decrease is not feasible without policy involvement. In fact, Scenarios 1 and 2 are even in contradiction to this desirable development, and show a strong increase.

This presents a major challenge for the European Union's transport policy based on the expected developments of the transport sector. In general two possibilities can be identified to meet this challenge of curbing CO_2 emissions by policy measures. Technological development (energy efficiency) can be stimulated and travel behavior can be steered in a more environmentally friendly direction. The implementation of fair and efficient pricing could be seen as a first step because environmental costs are included in prices. This will limit demand and probably create a modal shift towards more sustainable modes. However, it is doubtful whether the proposed initiatives are sufficient to reach the objectives in terms of emissions if we keep the various scenarios in mind. But policy changes and (unexpected) technological developments offer possibilities to achieve this objective.

CONCLUDING REMARKS

There is growing awareness that in the long term the development of society is characterized by substantial uncertainties. This often makes a prognosis-based approach inadequate. Scenario analysis is increasingly being used in long-range policy research, since it provides a way of identifying future issues and problems for policy making in an environment of qualitative uncertainty. Scenarios can be regarded as descriptions of possible futures that seem plausible under different sets of assumptions and provide a background against which policy assessments can be made. Scenarios are important tools for strategic policy analysis, especially in situations where policy makers have too much biased and unstructured information. The transport sector forms one of those fields where policy makers have to deal with many uncertainties as it is influenced by many factors. Despite these uncertainties, policy makers are faced with the objective of achieving sustainable mobility and need to have insight into future developments.

This paper presented possible future developments by sketching four European contrast images based on the outcome of earlier research. The outcome for the transport sector, expressed in transported volumes for both passenger and freight transport, was qualitatively described based on expected developments of several indicators. Developments in transport technology, spatial organization, distance and modals split have an impact on the transported volumes. This development was illustrated by indicators (+, 0, -) expressing the potential expected impact on modalities. This information formed the input for the calculation of CO_2 emissions with the focus on the EU. It appeared that for all four scenarios a decrease in emissions is not to be expected in 2020.

Sustainable mobility is central in current policy within the EU, this means the encouragement of the development of efficient and environmentally friendly transport systems that are safe and socially acceptable. In terms of emissions this means that a decrease is aimed at and needed in order to meet the Kyoto norm. The achievement of this target (sustainable mobility) seems difficult based on the outcomes presented in this paper. Several policy initiatives are needed to reach this ambitious target. It is doubtful whether the proposed measures by the EU are sufficient to bring about this decoupling in economic growth and emissions. But the implementation of efficient policy measures and (unexpected) technology developments might offer possibilities to make a step towards a more sustainable direction. Policy makers are thus faced with formidable policy challenges to achieve the Kyoto objectives in the next 20 years.

REFERENCES

1. CPB, 1999, Globalization, International Transport and the Global Environment: four quantitative scenarios, Working paper No. 110, The Hague
2. Department of Environment, Transport and the Regions (DETR), 1999, *Transport and the Economy, the Standing Advisory Committee on Trunk Road Assessment*, London
3. Dreborg, K.H., and P. Steen, 1994, *A Swedish Transportation Futures Study, Research Paper of the Environmental Strategies Research Group*, FMS, Stockholm
4. Commission of the European Communities, 1992, *The Future Development of the Common Transport Policy: A global approach to the Construction of a Community* Frameworefined astainable Mobility, Brussels.
5. European Communities, 1998, *Integrated Strategic Transport Infrastructure Networks in Europe*, Office for Official Publications of the European Communities, Luxembourg
6. Commission of the European Communities, 1998, *The Common Transport Policy - Sustainable Mobility: Perspectives for the Future*, Communication from the Commission to the Council, Brussels.
7. Geerlings, H., 1997, *Towards Sustainability of Technological Innovations in Transport*, Den Haag.
8. Masser, I., O. Sviden and M. Wegener, 1992, *The Geography of Europe's Futures*, Belhaven Press, London.
9. Nijkamp, P., and E. Blaas, 1994, *Impact assessment and Evaluation in Transportation Planning*, Kluwer, Dordrecht
10. Nijkamp, P., H. Ouwersloot and S.A. Rienstra, 1997, Sustainable Urban Transport Systems; An Expert-Based Strategic Scenario Approach, *Urban Studies*, vol. 34, no. 4, pp. 693-712.
11. Nijkamp, P., C.A. Rodenburg and B. Ubbels, 2000, *Transport Scenarios*, ESI, Free University, Amsterdam (to be published).
12. Olsthoorn, A.A., 2000, *Emissions*, IVM, Amsterdam (to be published).
13. Schafer, A. and D. Victor, 1997, The past and future of global mobility, *Scientific American*. Oct.

14. Van Veen-Groot, D.B., P. Nijkamp and J.C.J.M. van den Bergh, 1998-I, *Globalization, International Transport and the Global Environment, an assessment of trends and driving forces*, ESI, Free University, Amsterdam
15. Van Veen-Groot, D.B., and P. Nijkamp, 1999, *Globalization, International Transport and the Global Environment, a scenario approach*, ESI, Free University, Amsterdam
16. World Bank, 1996, *Global economic prospects and the developing countries*, Washington D.C., A World Bank Publication

Chapter 9

RESTRICTING WASTEFUL INTER-URBAN GOVERNMENT COMPETITION FOR PRIVATE-SECTOR INVESTMENT IN BRITAIN

Linda McCarthy
Department of Geography and Planning
The University of Toledo
Toledo, OH 43606-3390

INTRODUCTION

The [UK] prime minister is to intervene in an increasingly desperate government effort to prevent Nissan, the Japanese car maker, from switching production of its new Micra from Sunderland [England] to a French plant in the heart of the eurozone. Tony Blair and Stephen Byers, the trade and industry secretary, are to hold talks with Carlos Ghosn, Nissan president, at Downing Street later this month amid mounting ministerial and union fears that the new car will be built at Renault's Flins plant near Paris. Mr. Ghosn is a former executive at Renault where he earned a fearsome reputation as a cost cutter ... Nissan, in which Renault owns a 36.8% controlling stake, has already asked for UK state aid [thought to be in the order of £100 million] towards the £150 million investment it would have to make at Sunderland for the new Micra assembly line ... Even if they stump up money for Sunderland, ministers fear Nissan may follow the example of Toyota and go to France. That Japanese car maker, whose main European base is in Derbyshire [England], is building a new plant in Valenciennes, northern France, with substantial state aid (The Guardian (London) Newspaper, July 18, 2000).

The competition between cities for private-sector investment usually involves so-called "exogenous" development. Exogenous development results from "mobile" capital investment, such as a branch plant factory[1], that is attracted into a city from elsewhere. Local governments attempt to retain or attract such investment using incentives to businesses like grants, tax subsidies, and sites.

Determining the effectiveness of these urban entrepreneurial efforts depends on the scale of analysis. Much attention has been paid in the economic development literature to local government competition at the scale of individual cities. A substantial body of work, by development interests, government agencies, and related policy analysts, supports the provision of public incentives to companies (Cisneros 1995; Duckworth et al. 1986; European Commission 1992). This research contains case studies of particular cities that successfully attracted major companies and investment to their jurisdiction.

Another body of literature, by academics, community activists, and progressive planning professionals, identifies drawbacks for individual cities of competing for inward investment (Jensen-Butler et al. 1995; Jessop et al. 1996; Leitner and Sheppard 1998). These authors point to disadvantages associated with the enormous public resources diverted to companies as incentives, the inequitable distribution of the costs and benefits for different groups and areas within cities, and instances of fewer gains for local economies and residents than initially projected.

Less attention has been paid to the drawbacks of urban entrepreneurialism at the scale of systems of cities. Competition between local governments may be wasteful if it is zero or negative sum at a national or European Union (EU) scale of government: a company attracted to one city at public expense may merely represent investment lost to or redistributed from another (Bartik 1991; Kirby 1985).

In this paper, I examine two aspects of the competition for inward investment that have received comparatively little attention in the literature. First, I investigate the involvement of higher tiers of the state in restricting wasteful competition between local governments for the benefit of an urban system. I use the example of Britain[2] during the most recent Conservative government period, a time of considerable involvement in local economic development by higher tiers of the state. Second, I explore the opportunities for local governments to cooperate in the competition for private-sector investment, either in a bottom-up effort or in response to the stimulus of higher tiers of government.

RESTRICTING COMPETITION BETWEEN LOCAL GOVERNMENTS

A number of factors related to scale make regulating inter-urban competition difficult for higher tiers of the state. The different goals of the various scales of government can thwart efforts to minimize wasteful competition. The goal of national and EU tiers of government is to restrict the provision of public incentives that merely relocates companies within member states or the EU without any increase in employment or

---

[1] While not addressed in this paper, urban entrepreneurial efforts also typically include a focus on "endogenous" (intra-locally generated) economic development, such as new start-up businesses.

[2] Within Britain, the administrative structures and regulatory frameworks differ sufficiently to warrant a specific focus on England (Dicken, 1990; Johnston and Pattie, 1996).

productivity. In contrast, the aim of each local government's entrepreneurial efforts is to enhance the prosperity of its own particular jurisdiction. A local government can be sure to operate for the benefit of the larger national or supra-national economy only as a result of complying with regulations governing competition imposed by higher tiers of the state. Yet even with national and EU involvement, some local governments may attempt to operate solely for their individual advantage and may not comply with or even try to circumvent higher tier government regulation of competition.

Restricting wasteful competition at a lower scale of government will not eliminate it necessarily at higher scales. While British government efforts may curb wasteful competition nationally, competition between British cities and those in other West European countries can be wasteful at an EU scale. Another difficulty in limiting wasteful competition at a national or EU scale is that the restrictions may stymie the competitiveness of individual West European cities at a global scale. EU cities compete with cities elsewhere for international investment. When a company has not decided already to locate within the EU, it is counterproductive if national or EU restrictions on wasteful competition cause that company to locate somewhere else.

The British and EU levels of government intentionally and at times unintentionally restrict competition for inward investment between local governments. I investigate the extent to which these efforts minimize wasteful competition by examining the administrative structure, regulatory measures, and public subsidy schemes in England.

Administrative Structure

In the early 1990s, the British government modified its administrative structure at regional[3] and sub-regional[4] scales in England. At a regional level, the four primary national spending departments[5] were integrated in 1994 into one government office (GO) for each of the ten English regions. The goal was to coordinate the activities of the sub-regional units of government. The GOs represent the four main state departments in their dealings with local governments, private firms, and other organizations within each region. Many national policy decisions and funding allocations are now made at a regional level across these state departments (Rushbridge 1994).

Each GO seeks to enhance the prosperity of its own region by encouraging potential inward investors to locate within one of its local government jurisdictions. Every GO attempts to restrict wasteful competition within its own region so that local governments do not compete so vigorously with each other that a company can play one off against another and force up unnecessarily the incentives on offer. Yet because every GO is preoccupied with its own regional economy, each GO containing local governments with

---

[3] There are ten English regions: East, East Midlands, London, Merseyside (Liverpool), North East, North West, South East, South West, West Midlands, and Yorkshire and Humberside.

[4] Sub-regions (counties) usually have two tiers of elected government: county councils and local district councils.

[5] Environment, Trade and Industry, Employment and Education, and Transportation.

available sites can find itself in competition for the same inward investor with the GOs and local governments in other regions.

The British inward investment system is intended to restrict this kind of wasteful competition (Figure 1). At the apex of this nationally-coordinated hierarchical system is the Invest in Britain Bureau (IBB). The IBB acts as a promotional body that markets Britain internationally as a location for inward investment. The presumption is that the IBB is unbiased in terms of the site chosen for investment as long as it is somewhere within Britain (Dicken 1990). The IBB's role is to streamline the site selection process so that a potential company is offered only a select number of the optimum sites and incentive packages. The IBB attempts to restrict British cities from individually inundating potential companies with offers of incentives. National government is concerned that this type of competition could deter some investors because it creates an extremely confusing and time-consuming site selection process.

Figure 1 Hierarchical Structure of Inward Investment System in England

S   I

National: Invest in Britain Bureau (IBB)

T   (English Unit)   S

E   I S

↓   ↑   T

E

I   *Regional*: Regional Development Organizations (RDOs)

D   S

E   ⇓   ⇑   E

N   L

T   *Sub-Regional*: County Councils; quasi-public and promotional   E

I   organizations   C

F   T I

⇓   ⇑   E

E   D

D   *Local*: local governments; quasi-public and private-sector bodies

Source: author.

The IBB attempts to coordinate the activities of the five Regional Development Organizations[6] (RDOs) which compete with each other for potential investors. The RDOs are responsible for directing the overseas promotional activities of the sub-regional and local governments within their regions. The quality of such organization depends on the level of support for the RDO by these lower levels of government, which varies within and between regions (Dicken and Tickell 1992). The array of sub-regional and local

---

[6] Agency for Investment into North West England (INWARD), Northern Development Company (NDC), Yorkshire and Humberside Development Association (YHDA), West Midlands Industrial Development Association (WMIDA), Devon and Cornwall Development Bureau (DCDB).

public, quasi-public, and private bodies involved in promoting cities to potential investors complicates coordination efforts.

At a sub-regional scale, county councils promote their sub-region as a location for private-sector investment. A number of counties, particularly where the county council has been abolished, established economic development agencies[7] to attract inward investment to the county. Finally, at a local level, a multitude of agencies including local governments, Urban Development Corporations (UDCs), and New Town Development Corporations compete for private investment.

While their major source of funding is the IBB, the RDOs receive subscriptions from sub-regional and local governments, private businesses, and other groups within their regions (Dicken 1990). In order to receive national funding, the RDOs must satisfy the IBB's requirements to coordinate lower level agencies' promotional efforts and to identify the optimum British site for each potential investor. At the same time, to secure local contributions, the RDOs must attempt to satisfy or at least consider each local government's desire for inward investment.

The national inward investment system is set up so that the initial inquiry from a potential investor comes to the IBB (Figure 1). The IBB channels the inquiry to the RDOs, which in turn pass it along to the sub-regional bodies including the county councils and economic development agencies, which then transmit the inquiry to local agencies such as the local governments and UDCs. Within this hierarchy, the lower level bodies put forward their own most suitable sites. At each level up the hierarchy, these locations are narrowed down to a small number of the most attractive sites and incentive packages from which the potential investor can choose.

This inward investment system appears to reflect a coherent national policy. It attempts to restrict free-for-all competition. The system does not eliminate competition altogether, however, because at each level of the hierarchy, places compete for each potential investor. The hierarchical nature of this system initially places local governments in competition with each other at a sub-regional level. The smaller number of local governments with attractive incentive packages that survive the site selection process at this sub-regional stage then enter the competition at a regional level.

Due to cost constraints, most local governments entrust their overseas marketing to their RDO. In accepting this largely reactive role[8], local governments are dependent on higher tiers of the hierarchical inward investment system for information and consequently for their ultimate success or failure in securing foreign investment. There is no mechanism in place, however, to prevent an individual local government from enjoying the benefits of this quite reactive system while also proactively attempting to attract foreign investment on its own. A small number of local governments already directly market themselves internationally. Following its selection in the 1980s as the location for a Nissan car assembly plant employing about 4,500 workers, Sunderland promoted itself overseas as a location for automotive investment (Sunderland

---

[7] For example, the Tyne and Wear Economic Development Company (TWEDCO) was established in Tyneside after the Tyne and Wear Metropolitan County Council was abolished in 1986.

[8] Local governments are more proactive when they receive a direct inquiry from an investor.

Metropolitan City Council 1996). The concern of national government officials about this type of entrepreneurial activity is that a company might initially welcome Sunderland's incentive offer, and then use it to play different areas off against each other to increase the public subsidies on offer (GO North East 1996).

Beginning in the late-1980s, the British government modified its administrative structure at a sub-regional scale in England. Until 1987, England had a two-tier elected local government structure: county councils and local district councils. The county councils comprised a small number of metropolitan councils and a larger number of shire councils. In 1987, the Greater London Council (GLC) and the six metropolitan county councils were replaced by unitary all-purpose local district councils[9]. In 1992, the British government began to replace the remaining two-tier structures with one tier of local government. A lack of public support and conflicts between the interest groups representing the two tiers of local government resulted in only a small number of county councils being abolished and replaced by a unitary local district council (Johnston and Pattie 1996).

The abolition of some county councils, however, removed the only elected level of government with a concern for the overall well-being of these particular counties. This situation could increase the potential for wasteful competition because each local government within these counties may now operate solely for its own benefit and without regard for the prosperity of their county as a whole. In some counties, however, the unitary local governments and other quasi-public and private bodies established countywide economic development agencies[10]. Joint funding for an economic development agency and overseas promotion, however, is motivated by individual self-interest rather than a concern for the benefit of the sub-region and a desire for substantive cooperation.

Generally, it is easier for local and sub-regional governments to act on their own behalf and compete individually for private investment than to cooperate with other governments. Indeed, Harding and Garside (1995, 182) identified that:

> The record of voluntary cooperation across local administrative boundaries is not good ... [with] ... few historical reasons to suggest they [the GOs] will do much more than referee inter-authority conflicts ... [so] ... local authorities will compete more and more aggressively with each other for public and private resources.

---

[9] While the stated goal was to remove duplicated functions and spending, this move was viewed as a political act - a response to local Labour Councils' "high spending" and attempts to use local government as a welfare vehicle in opposition to central workfare policies (Pickvance, 1991).

[10] Such as TWEDCO.

Regulatory Measures

A prominent feature of the Conservative government's regulatory environment was the tight national control, for economic as well as political reasons[11], of local revenue generation and expenditure for economic development. Central control of local government revenue raising capacity included the local business property tax regime that was introduced in 1990. The Uniform Business Rate was fixed at, collected, and redistributed from the center. This kind of tax regime affected inter-urban competition for private-sector investment in unintended ways. It removed a major motivation for local entrepreneurial activity that is found in the US: increasing the local property tax base.

Harding (1990, 98) argued that this tax system would "reduce the incentive for authorities to promote economic growth, since the fiscal benefit accrued locally will no longer be significant" and that "local governments have no incentive to do anything extra for business since it is community-charge payers who will have to pay for it all unless special charges are introduced." Harding (1990, 93) concluded that this nationalization of the local business tax would "break the link between local development policy and fiscal health" and "give far greater freedom to local government *not* to operate business-friendly strategies." This scenario did not happen, however, because, in contrast to the US, cities in England, especially those located in high unemployment traditional manufacturing areas, compete for private investment to increase jobs more than tax base.

Changes in national regeneration funding application procedures in the early 1990s promoted a culture of competition for *public* funds. Central government forced local governments in England to compete in a system where allocations were no longer based on need but on a city's perceived potential to most effectively spend the funds (Robson et al. 1994; Harding and Garside 1995; Ward 1997)[12]. Similarly in 1995, the EU approved a competitive bidding requirement for about 5 percent of its regional funds for England. Consequently, local governments in England were no longer competing with each other only for private investment, but for national and EU funding as well.

Central government traditionally also tightly controlled local government expenditure on economic development. Despite the absence of a legislative basis providing specific local powers to engage in economic development spending until 1989, local governments creatively used general powers available to them. Section 137 of the 1972 Local Government Act was used extensively, especially in less prosperous areas. Section 137 gives a local government blanket right to spend up to the product of a two penny rate for any purpose beneficial to all or part of its population.

Despite such creative measures, local government direct spending on economic development remained extremely limited. One unintended effect of this restricted local

---

[11] Thatcher government centralization efforts tried to reduce local expenditures, limit spending on the social agendas of labor-oriented local Labour governments, and "punish opposition parties while rewarding their own supporters" (Goldsmith and Newton, 1988, 363).

[12] I mention this competition for *public* funds as further evidence of the growing culture of competition in Britain. Competing for *public* funding, however, differs conceptually and practically from the competition for *private* funds (see McCarthy 2000).

spending capacity was to constrain inter-urban competition that depended exclusively on locally-generated financial inducements. Instead, cities resorted to offering non-financial subsidies to companies, such as sites and transportation infrastructure.

With the 1989[13] Local Government and Housing Act, central government granted local governments specific powers to engage in economic development efforts for the first time. Local governments could "participate in or encourage the setting up or expansion of any commercial, industrial or public undertaking as long as it lay within the authority's area and was likely to increase or protect employment opportunities for local residents" (Harding and Garside 1995, 168). The national government maintained control, however, by requiring local governments to publish annual economic development plans containing expenditure proposals for central review, and reserved extensive powers of veto (Harding 1990). Although not free to pursue agendas opposed to central goals, local governments now had more potential to compete with each other for private investment using local funds.

Public Subsidy

The EU and Britain regulate the provision of public incentive packages to businesses. EU Competition Policy[14] contains a general ban on state aids such as subsidies and grants. In theory, this prohibits competition for private investment using public funds. In practice, Competition Policy allows state aids to companies to promote development in areas with low living standards or serious under-employment (European Commission 1986)[15]. Depending on the severity of need, cities are permitted to provide state aids to firms up to a pre-established percentage of total project cost (75 percent in "backward" regions[16] and 30 percent in "declining industrial" areas[17]).

Within Britain, Competition Policy allows state aids to private enterprises in the economically-weakest areas, which are largely outside the southeast of England. Competition Policy, however, does not minimize wasteful competition between needy local governments within England or the EU as a whole. Cities in "backward" regions compete with each other and with cities in "declining industrial" regions for private investment by endeavoring to offer up to the maximum of 75 percent of a project's cost in state aids. Cities in "declining industrial" regions compete with each other and with

---

[13] Local Labour governments developed a more pragmatic approach to central government policy with the end of the general use of Section 137 with this Act, the 1987 Conservative national election victory, and the abolition of the metropolitan county councils and GLC in 1986 (Harding and Garside, 1995).

[14] Article 92(1), 1957 EEC Treaty.

[15] State aids are also permitted for small and medium sized enterprises across the EU.

[16] The Objective 1 or "backward" regions are the most deprived due to problems associated with their peripherality, sparse population, economic structure, or poor endowment of infrastructure.

[17] The Objective 2 regions are undergoing "industrial restructuring." They have an economic structure that is overly dependent on one or a small number of traditional industries such as coal or shipbuilding and face serious unemployment and economic restructuring problems.

cities in the "backward" regions, by offering up to 30 percent of a project's cost to investors[18].

As in most European countries, the British government provides financial aid to help attract companies to its most needy areas. The nationally-designated Assisted Areas represent the most deprived areas within the EU's "backward" and "declining industrial" areas. The Assisted Areas comprise Development Areas (DAs) and Intermediate Areas (IAs) where national state aids to firms may be available up to a limit of 30 percent and 20 percent of the project cost respectively.

The British government's Regional Selective Assistance (RSA)[19] represents the bulk of the financial incentives for major firms within the Assisted Areas. Central government controls the involvement of lower tiers of the state in inward investment then, not only with the IBB's inward investment hierarchical system, but also by controlling much of the financial expenditure used as incentives. RSA allocations to firms are completely "selective" on the part of central government. Local governments apply for these national subsidies to attract investment, and each firm individually negotiates with national government for its RSA allocation (Dicken 1990).

The nationally-implemented RSA scheme minimizes wasteful competition involving public subsidy to firms within the least prosperous areas of England because it allows up to the same amount of RSA to all local governments within similarly-designated Assisted Areas[20]. This removes the potential for a firm to be attracted to one DA or IA versus another simply to secure a larger RSA award.

Nonetheless, the RSA scheme does not eliminate wasteful competition. National government sanctions each GO to provide up to £2 million in RSA without central authorization. This increases the opportunity for inter-regional competition using RSA in conjunction with other local incentives. Furthermore, RSA may promote competition between similarly-designated local areas because they may be more likely to compete with each other simply because they can offer this potential national source of funds to attract investment. In contrast, local governments in the US typically must put together incentive packages that have a higher percentage of local financial assistance.

Do EU and British Restrictions Address Criticisms of Inter-Urban Competition?

Having examined the intended and unintended ways that higher tiers of government restrict wasteful competition between cities, it is worth considering briefly the extent to which these restrictions address some of the drawbacks of competition for private investment that have been identified in the literature. One criticism of inter-urban competition is that, instead of creating new jobs, the efforts of individual local

---

[18] British city governments compete with each other and with those across the EU and further afield.

[19] Section 7, Industry Act 1982 (formerly the Industry Act 1972).

[20] Although not always accomplished in practice, RSA is not intended for merely relocating employment from elsewhere in Britain to the Assisted Areas.

governments to secure inward investment are wasteful because they merely redistribute jobs between competing areas at considerable public expense (Bartik 1991; Kirby 1985). Although state aids do redistribute employment, higher tiers of the state in Western Europe use these funds to steer jobs to the economically-weakest areas where they are most needed.

Another criticism of competition is that it benefits already-prosperous cities that either do not need to offer any or can afford to offer enormous incentives to private firms. EU Competition Policy, however, permits only the economically-weakest areas to provide state aids to companies to improve their competitive advantage. A further criticism of competition is that state aids promote inefficient companies that are dependent on public subsidy. Within the EU, where state aids are restricted to the economically-weakest areas, the incentives provided to companies are viewed as offsetting the disadvantages associated with locating in these usually peripheral less prosperous areas.

COOPERATION BETWEEN LOCAL GOVERNMENTS

In addition to examining EU and British efforts to regulate wasteful competition, it is useful to consider the potential for local governments to cooperate in the competition for private-sector investment. Western Europe has a well-established tradition of cooperative efforts between local governments to secure both public and private funds.

Cooperation to Secure Public Funds

Many urban cooperative networks in Western Europe focus on lobbying higher tiers of government for *public* funding for economic development. For example, Eurocities is a forum for more than two dozen "second cities" like Rotterdam, Barcelona, Birmingham, Frankfurt, Milan, and Lyon. Eurocities was founded in a bottom-up effort in 1986 at a conference in Rotterdam but now obtains funds from the EU to support programs that include information and best practice exchange (Borja 1992; European Commission, n.d; Leitner and Sheppard 1999; Marlow 1992). In contrast, the cooperative networks in the Regions and Cities of Europe (RECITE) Pilot Project for Innovate Action were established in response to an EU top-down initiative. Since 1991, the EU has funded nearly forty RECITE networks that promote the economic development and competitiveness of member cities (European Commission, n.d.).

Cities often join these networks to secure funding from higher tiers of the state for specific cross-jurisdictional programs and projects. These cooperative efforts, however, usually involve relatively straightforward cooperative bidding for national or EU funds that enhance local competitiveness through joint research and development, education and training, or infrastructure projects like roads and bridges. It is relatively easy to achieve this type of cooperation to secure public funding because the costs and benefits of cooperation are clearly discernible for each project or program.

Some researchers argue that top-down efforts to promote cooperation, however, can produce more permanent cooperative working relationships in the longer term (European Commission 1992). Yet the same cities that cooperate to secure public funds may have no qualms about entering into cut-throat competition with each other for a private investor that is considering locating in only one of their jurisdictions. In fact, Guisinger (1985) identified that inter-national competition for inward investment is particularly strong between countries that belong to a common market.

Cooperation to Attract Private-Sector Investment

Cooperative networks between cities to attract *private* investment typically involve joint place marketing and perhaps tax base sharing. For example, the Communauté Urbaine de Lille (CUdL) is a network of 86 local governments with joint regional decision-making for the Lille metropolitan region of France. The CUdL introduced a tax base sharing agreement, the Fonds de Développement Economique et Solidaire and uses the funds to promote economic development within the region. Mechanisms to discourage individual local governments from operating outside the joint regional decision-making framework include the "25% measure." A local government that independently develops an industrial estate, for instance, must transfer 25 percent of the taxes on the estate to the CUdL (van den Berg and van Klink 1995; van den Berg et al. 1993).

This type of cooperation can potentially increase inward investment because the region as a whole can be marketed overseas more effectively and less expensively. A particular city may not be well-known internationally, but its region may be large enough to be familiar already to foreign firms. These intra-metropolitan cooperative networks, however, involve a limited number of local government within a contiguous region. Unless endogenous development and economic specialization between regions occurs, this kind of cooperation will eliminate competition only between the locally-cooperating jurisdictions within particular regions. The drawbacks of competition that apply at a local scale will not be eliminated but will be replicated at a regional scale. The competition for exogenous development between regions does not guarantee a more efficient or productive national or EU economy any more than the competition between local governments does (Leitner and Sheppard 1999).

Rather, cooperation between the non-contiguous local governments across Western Europe is necessary in order to address the zero sum nature of competition at national and EU scales. This kind of cooperation would potentially control the level of incentives offered to companies because it could prevent investors from playing one city off against another to increase the public subsidies on offer. Such cooperative competition would be particularly effective when a potential company has already determined that it needs to locate somewhere within the EU.

Even in the US, there has been recent acknowledgment that individual cities locked into competition with each other results in publicly-subsidized private projects that would have been built anyway. Molotch and Logan (1985, 160) have called for cities to cooperate because:

> these efforts are best waged not by particular cities in isolation from one another, but as part of a program that recognizes how the system of cities actually works and how its destructive tendencies can be defeated through coordinated actions across urban areas. In essence, U.S. cities must stop competing among themselves for capital and use their relatively high level of legal autonomy to compete as a collective force against the growth machine system that has captured them all.

The drawback of this suggestion is that, even if cooperation is at the scale of a system of cities, the mechanism for achieving it remains at the individual local scale. Each city must unilaterally seek to cooperate with all other local areas. Such bottom-up initiated cooperative competition is unlikely. Acting individually, one or a small number of local governments, even if they wanted to, cannot resist competing out of fear that other cities may continue to do so and attract the available investment.

This kind of collective inaction has been analyzed as a tragedy of the commons or a prisoners' dilemma. The classic example of the tragedy of the commons involves a group of herders and a public pasture where rational individual decisions lead to an irrational group outcome (Hardin 1968). Each herder individually gets the greatest guaranteed benefit by grazing as many animals as possible in the common area. Yet as a group, they create a collective disaster that is foreseeable and even preventable: the individual actions of all the herders will exceed the carrying capacity of the pasture which will become overgrazed and unavailable for grazing by anyone.

Theories of cooperation, including iterated game theory and the well-known prisoners' dilemma game, provide insights into this collective inaction problem. In the simple two-person game, each player chooses between two options, to "defect" or to "cooperate," without regard for the decision of the other. The best outcome for both players will occur if they both choose to cooperate. A less optimum overall outcome results if one player cooperates and the other defects. The worst outcome for both players occurs if they both defect. Yet the strategy chosen by each player will be to defect because neither can guarantee that the other will cooperate (Ostrom 1990).

So, while local governments may agree that eliminating wasteful and expensive competition for private investment is a preferable outcome for the group as a whole, the actual outcome will be mutual defection. Each local government will act in its own interest and defect when it gets the opportunity to attract a company by offering public incentives because it cannot be certain that other local governments will do otherwise.

The problems of cooperation increase with the size of the cooperating group. For the large number of local governments across the EU urban system, there are enormous "organization costs" to be overcome in the areas of communication and bargaining (Olson 1971). The difficulties for individual cities of resolving the combination and levels of incentives for each project make cooperation a logistical nightmare. The unavoidable need to determine the benefits of cooperation, such as increased employment and property taxes for each locality (for political as well as economic reasons) is formidable. The potential company cannot physically set up in all of the cooperating jurisdictions and must inevitably locate within only one, or at best, on the boundary of a small number of jurisdictions.

Recognizing the difficulties of achieving binding and effective bottom-up initiated cooperation, Ostrom (1990, 16) suggested that members of a cooperative network could organize themselves by hiring "a private agent to take on the role of enforcer." A more likely option in Western Europe would be for higher levels of government to promote cooperation. Yet while some authors believe that the prisoners' dilemma represents a convincing argument for the involvement of higher tiers of the state, others believe that this is not necessary or argue against it. Taylor (1987, 168-170) maintained that:

> the more the state intervenes in such situations, the more 'necessary' (in this view) it becomes, because positive altruism and voluntary cooperative behavior *atrophy* in the presence of the state and *grow* in its absence. Thus, again, the state exacerbates the conditions which are supposed to make it necessary. We might say that the state is like an addictive drug: the more of it we have, the more we 'need' it and the more we come to 'depend' on it ... Under the state, there is no *practice* of cooperation and no growth of a sense of the interdependence on which cooperation depends; there are fewer opportunities for the spontaneous expression of direct altruism and there are therefore fewer altruistic acts to be observed, with the result that there is no growth of the feeling of assurance that others around one are altruistic or at least willing to behave cooperatively - an assurance that one will not be let down if one tries unilaterally to cooperate.

Yet in the absence of unilateral bottom-up cooperation, the existing system of competition works in favor of private firms and at the expense of cities and their residents. And there is some potential for higher tiers of the state to promote cooperation and create an environment in which the benefits are shared so that further cooperation becomes desirable. This is particularly relevant within the EU policy context where higher tiers of the state already promote cooperative networks of various kinds across a number of countries. Of course, issues of scale, and recognition of the greater need for investment within the "backward" and "declining industrial regions" would need to be addressed through the EU's regional policy and funding framework.

Higher tiers of the state can attempt to distribute the costs and benefits of cooperation evenly over time and between cooperating jurisdictions. In a system that "spreads" the investment among cooperating areas, there is greater certainty for individual local areas that they will receive a share of total inward investment. In terms of the self-interest of the local areas themselves, advantages include channeling some of the public funds that are not provided as incentives into more productive activities such as improving the skills of the labor force. This type of productive investment can contribute to more sustainable economic development and may even help these cities remain competitive against other places outside Western Europe that instead channel their resources into incentive packages.

Higher tiers of government can appeal to and promote those local factors that are important for active cooperation. Social capital has been identified as a vital component in successful cooperative efforts (Ostrom 1990; Putnam 1993). Stocks of social capital include accounts of trust and social and professional norms. A certain level of trust is necessary for individual voluntary cooperation to replace mutual defection when the possibility to defect for short-term guaranteed benefits is open to all. Accounts of trust are built up through repeated instances of cooperation that generate greater trust and further cooperation (Putnam 1993). The development of stronger social and professional norms governing cooperative behavior has also been identified as important in achieving successful cooperation. Members of a group conform to an accepted norm for altruistic reasons like wanting to live up to certain ideals or in order to avoid negative repercussions like a loss of reputation or self respect (Taylor 1987).

There is also the option for higher tiers of the state to work with local governments to adopt and enforce sanctions against "defectors." These penalties could include a "100 percent measure" - a more punitive version of the forfeiture system for defectors adopted by the CUdL in Lille.

CONCLUDING COMMENTS

A company can hold a city hostage by threatening to leave if it does not receive demanded incentives like tax breaks and subsidies. A business that is considering moving to a new location can play one city off against another in order to drive up the level of public inducements on offer.

While the competition for private-sector investment between local governments has been the focus on much research in the economic development literature, limited attention has been paid to the involvement of higher tiers of the state in restricting competition between local governments for the benefit of an urban system. Similarly, inadequate attention has been paid to cooperation between the local governments across Europe in the competition for private-sector investment. Research on urban cooperative networks in Europe has concentrated instead primarily on either cooperation between contiguous and non-contiguous cities to secure public funding and other considerations from higher tiers of the state or cooperation by cities within the same region to promote private inward investment and limit wasteful competition.

Further research is needed at the scale of the European urban system that explores the opportunities and challenges associated with both restricting wasteful competition for inward investment and promoting cooperation between these non-contiguous local governments in the competition for companies and the economic activity and jobs that they generate. This research focus is significant not only as a scholarly endeavor but also because the public policy and budgetary implications of this analysis have a direct bearing on the economic prosperity of European cities and their residents.

ACKNOWLEDGMENTS

I would like to thank Eric Sheppard, University of Minnesota, and Andy Jonas, University of Hull, for their helpful comments on earlier versions of this paper.

REFERENCES

1. Bartik, T. J. (1991) *Who Benefits from State and Local Economic Development Policies?* W. E. Upjohn Institute for Employment Research, Kalamazoo.
2. Borja, J. (1992) Eurocities - A system of major urban centers in Europe. *Ekistics* 59:352/353, 21-27.
3. Cisneros, Henry G. (1995) *Urban Entrepreneurialism and National Economic Growth.* Washington, DC: US Department of Housing and Urban Development.
4. Dicken, P. (1990) Seducing Foreign Investors - The Competitive Bidding Strategies of Local and Regional Agencies in the United Kingdom. In M. Hebbert and J. C. Hansen (eds.) *Unfamiliar Territory: The Reshaping of European Geography.* Avebury, Aldershot, 162-88.
5. _____ and A. Tickell (1992) Competitors or Collaborators? The Structure of Inward Investment Promotion in Northern England. *Regional Studies,* 26:1, 99-106.
6. Duckworth, R., J. Simmons, and R. McNulty (1986) *The Entrepreneurial American City.* Partners for Livable Places, Washington, DC.
7. European Commission (1992) Urbanisation and the Functions of Cities in the European Community. European Commission, Brussels.
8. _____ (1986) *National Regional Development Aid.* Information and Publications Division of the European Communities, Brussels.
9. _____ (n.d.) *Urban Pilot Projects.* second edition, Office for Official Publications of the European Communities, Luxembourg.
10. Goldsmith, M. and K. Newton (1988) Centralisation and decentralisation: changing patterns of intergovernmental relations in advanced western societies. *European Journal of Political Research,* 16, 359-363.
11. GO (Government Office) North East (UK) (1996) Interview with Tony Dell, Director, Trade, Industry and Europe Directorate, January.
12. Guisinger, S. (ed.) (1985) Investment Incentives and Performance Requirements. Praeger, New York.
13. Hardin, G. (1968) The tragedy of the commons. *Science,* 162, 1243-1248.
14. Harding, A. (1990) Local Autonomy and Urban Economic Development Policies: The Recent UK Experience in Perspective. In D. S. King and J. Pierre (eds.) *Challenges to Local Government.* Sage, London, 78-100.
15. _____ and P. Garside (1995) Urban and Economic Development. In J. Stewart and G. Stoker (eds.) *Local Government in the 1990s.* Macmillan, Basingstoke, 166-87.
16. Jensen-Butler, C., A. Shachar, and J. van Weesep (eds.) (1997) *European Cities in Competition.* Avebury, Aldershot.

17. Jessop, R., J. Peck, and A. Tickell (1996) *Retooling the machine: economic crisis, state restructuring, and urban politics*. Paper presented at the Association of American Geographers Annual Meeting, Charlotte, NC, April.

18. Johnston, R. J. and C. J. Pattie (1996) Local Government in Local Governance: the 1994-95 Restructuring of Local Government in England. *International Journal of Urban and Regional Research,* 20:4, 671-96.

19. Kirby, A. (1985) Nine Fallacies of Local Economic Change. *Urban Affairs Quarterly*, 21:2, 207-20.

20. Leitner, H. and E. Sheppard (1999) Transcending Interurban Competition: Conceptual Issues and Policy Alternatives in the European Union. In A. E. G. Jonas and D. Wilson (eds.) *The Urban Growth Machine: Critical Perspectives Twenty Years Later.* SUNY Press, Albany, 227-243.

21. _____ (1998) Economic Uncertainty, Inter-Urban Competition and the Efficacy of Entrepreneurialism. In T. Hall and P. Hubbard (eds.) *The Entrepreneurial City: Geographies of Politics, Regime and Representation.* Wiley, Chichester, 285-307.

22. Marlow, D. (1992) Eurocities: From urban networks to a European Urban Policy. *Ekistics* 59:352/353, 28-32.

23. McCarthy, L. (2000) The Changing Culture of Inter-Urban Government Competition in Britain. *Applied Geography Papers and Proceedings.* 23, forthcoming.

24. Molotch, H. and J. R. Logan (1985) Urban Dependencies: New Forms of Use and Exchange in U.S. Cities. *Urban Affairs Quarterly,* 21:2, 143-69.

25. Olson, M. (1971) The Logic of Collective Action: Public Goods and the Theory of Groups. Cambridge: Harvard University Press.

26. Ostrom, E. (1990) Governing the Commons: The evolution of institutions for collective action. Cambridge: Cambridge University Press.

27. Pickvance, C. (1991) The difficulty of control and the ease of structural reform: British local government in the 1980s. In C. Pickvance and E. Preteceille (eds.) *State restructuring and local power: A comparative perspective.* Pinter, London, 48-89.

28. Putnam, R. D. (1993) The Prosperous Community: Social Capital and Public Life. *The American Prospect*, 13, 35-42.

29. Robson, B., M. Bradford, I. Deas, E. Hall, E. Harrison, M. Parkinson, R. Evans, P. Garside, A. Harding, and F. Robinson (1994) *Assessing The Impact of Urban Policy.* HMSO, London.

30. Rushbridge, B. (ed.) (1994) *Municipal Year Book 1994.* Municipal Journal Ltd., London.

31. Sunderland Metropolitan City Council (UK) (1996) Interview with Tom Hurst, Principal Executive Officer, Marketing and Economic Development Department, January.

32. Taylor, M. (1987) *The Possibility of Cooperation.* Cambridge University Press, Cambridge.

33. van den Berg, L., and H. A. van Klink (1995) Regional competition, city marketing and strategic urban networks. In P. Cheshire and I. R. Gordon (eds.) *Territorial Competition in an Integrating Europe.* Avebury, Aldershot, 206-221.

34. van den Berg, L., H. A. van Klink, and J. van der Meer (1993) *Governing Metropolitan Regions*. Aldershot: Avebury.
35. Ward, K. G. (1997) Coalitions in urban regeneration: a regime approach. *Environment and Planning A*, 29, 1493-1506.

INDEX